HISTORY OF CRIME AND PUNISHMENT

THE HISTORY OF LAW ENFORCEMENT

BY DUCHESS HARRIS, JD, PHD

WITH REBECCA MORRIS

Essential Library

An Imprint of Abdo Publishing | abdobooks.com

ABDOBOOKS.COM

Published by Abdo Publishing, a division of ABDO, PO Box 398166, Minneapolis, Minnesota 55439. Copyright © 2020 by Abdo Consulting Group, Inc. International copyrights reserved in all countries. No part of this book may be reproduced in any form without written permission from the publisher. Essential Library™ is a trademark and logo of Abdo Publishing.

Printed in the United States of America, North Mankato, Minnesota.
022019
092019

THIS BOOK CONTAINS RECYCLED MATERIALS

Interior Photos: Gerald Herbert/AP Images, 5; Mark Mulligan/Houston Chronicle/AP Images, 7; David Carson/St. Louis Post-Dispatch/AP Images, 11; Eric Gay/AP Images, 12; North Wind Picture Archives, 17, 18, 38; C. M. Bell/C. M. Bell Studio Collection/Library of Congress, 21; Bain News Service/George Grantham Bain Collection/Library of Congress, 25; AP Images, 29, 30, 49, 65, 69; MPI/Archive Photos/Getty Images, 32; Brian Zak/Sipa Press/madoff_bz.005/0911131952/AP Images, 40–41; Lynne Sladky/AP Images, 44; John Roman Images/Shutterstock Images, 52–53; Nicholas Kamm/AFP/Getty Images, 55; Bettmann/Getty Images, 56; WX/AP Images, 70; Douglas C. Pizac/AP Images, 73; Jim Collins/AP Images, 77; Diane Bondareff/AP Images, 78; Ted S. Warren/AP Images, 82; Robert Nickelsberg/Getty Images News/Getty Images, 85; iStockphoto, 88–89; Susan Walsh/AP Images, 90; Silvia Flores/The Fresno Bee/AP Images, 92–93; Ted S. Warren/AP Images, 97

Editor: Charly Haley
Series Designer: Dan Peluso

LIBRARY OF CONGRESS CONTROL NUMBER: 2018966014

PUBLISHER'S CATALOGING-IN-PUBLICATION DATA

Names: Harris, Duchess, author | Morris, Rebecca, author.
Title: The history of law enforcement / by Duchess Harris and Rebecca Morris
Description: Minneapolis, Minnesota: Abdo Publishing, 2020 | Series: History of crime and punishment | Includes online resources and index.
Identifiers: ISBN 9781532119200 (lib. bdg.) | ISBN 9781532173387 (ebook)
Subjects: LCSH: Law enforcement--United States--History--Juvenile literature. | Police--United States--History--Juvenile literature. | Criminal justice, Administration of--United States--History--Juvenile literature.
Classification: DDC 363.20973--dc23

CONTENTS

CHAPTER ONE

A SHOOTING ATTACK IN DALLAS

Dallas police officers comfort each other the day after a shooting killed five officers in their city.

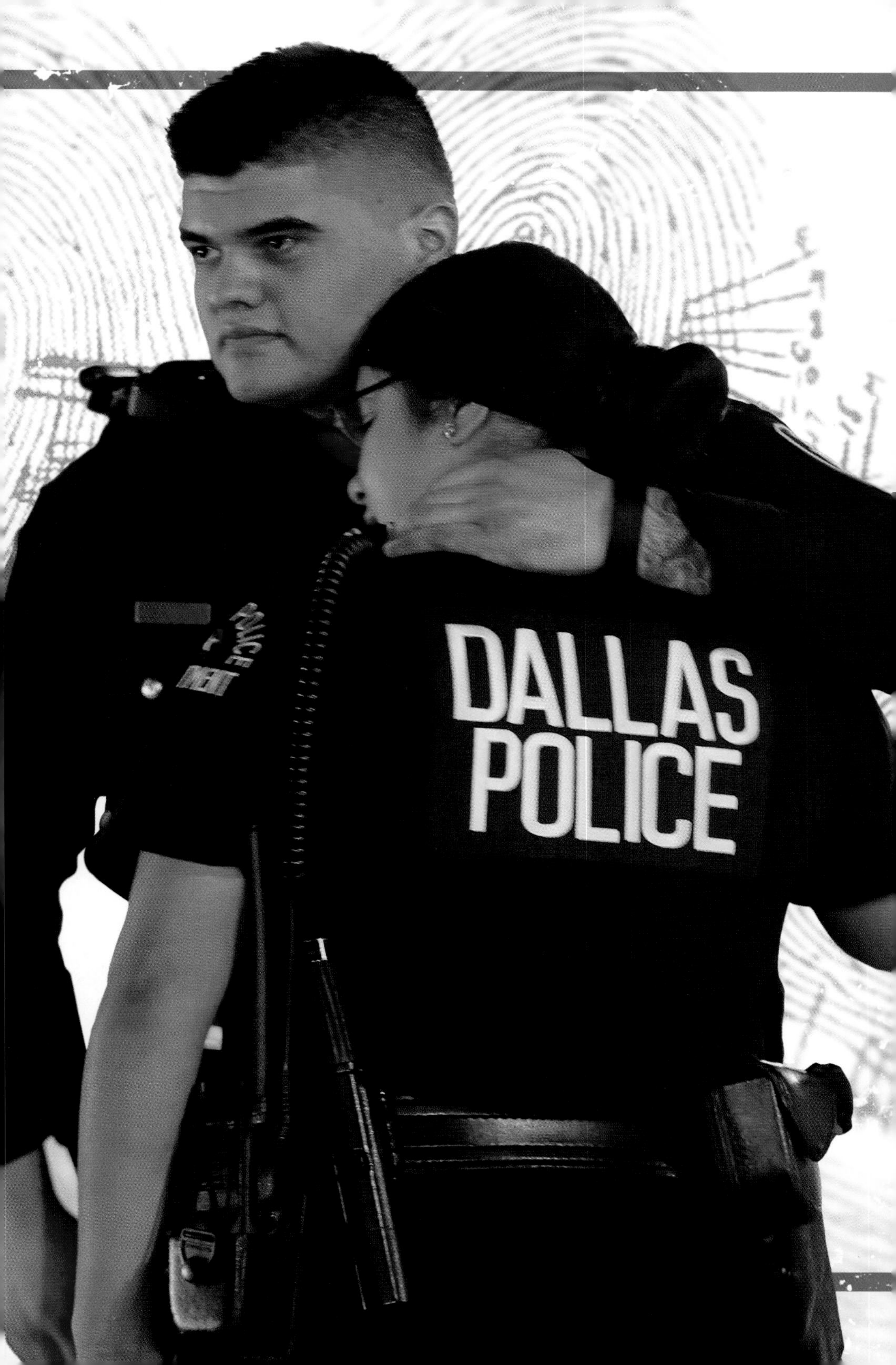
DALLAS
POLICE

Just before 1:30 a.m. on July 8, 2016, law enforcement officers in Dallas, Texas, used a robot armed with explosives to kill 25-year-old Micah Johnson. His death came hours after he fatally shot four officers of the Dallas Police Department (DPD) and one officer of the Dallas Area Rapid Transit (DART) Police. Johnson's gunfire also wounded seven other officers and two civilians. The attack occurred at a public protest that had been organized to address the problem of police brutality. Johnson was not one of the protest's participants.

Protesters had gathered in the streets to voice their anger over the deaths of Alton Sterling in Louisiana and Philando Castile in Minnesota. Both Sterling and Castile were black men, and their deaths were the latest in a series of shootings that drew attention to law enforcement's use of deadly force against people of color. Almost 100 law enforcement officers monitored the protest to ensure that it would remain peaceful.

Johnson began shooting just as the protest was ending. He wore a bulletproof vest and was carrying three guns, including a high-powered assault-style rifle. At first, Johnson fired in the street. He concentrated on an area where police officers were blocking traffic as a safety precaution to protect protesters. Three officers were fatally shot in that initial gunfire. Other officers carried the wounded to emergency vehicles, directed civilians to run for cover, and shielded bystanders. Next, Johnson entered a nearby El Centro College building. Officers working for the college were stationed inside. Johnson shot and wounded the officers, but they were able to prevent him from getting farther into the building. Johnson continued moving through the street, where he approached a DART officer and shot him at close range several times. That officer died. Johnson was then able to find another way to enter the El Centro College building. He positioned himself at a second-floor window

Officers guard the scene of the fatal shooting attack in downtown Dallas in 2016.

SHETAMIA TAYLOR'S PERSPECTIVE

Shetamia Taylor was one of two civilians wounded in the Dallas shooting. She was at the protest with her four sons, who were 12, 14, 15, and 18 at the time. When the shooting began, Taylor told her sons to run, and they were separated in the chaos. Taylor had one son with her when she was shot in her leg. Officers surrounded them and shielded them until it was safe to get to a car and drive to the hospital. Another of Taylor's sons, Kavion, remembers an officer who helped him run to safety: "He was really selfless and put himself in harm's way to protect us."[2] After seeing the officers' actions during the shooting, Taylor's youngest son, Jermar, wants to be a police officer when he grows up. Since the shooting, Taylor has struggled with recovery, but she has also been active in the community. She is involved with the Texas Organizing Project, a group that advocates for black and Hispanic communities on a range of issues such as health care, education, and financial security. She has also participated in educational talks and panels on race and community, and she has forged friendships with members of law enforcement.

and resumed shooting, aiming down into the street. Another police officer was killed from those gunshots.

About 20 minutes after Johnson's attack began, law enforcement confronted him in the El Centro College building. They used a trained crisis negotiator to try to convince him to surrender peacefully. During the negotiations, Johnson stated his motivation for the shooting. Dallas police chief David Brown reported, "He said he was upset about the recent police shootings. The suspect said he was upset at white people. The suspect stated he wanted to kill white people, especially white officers."[1] Johnson refused to surrender. He mentioned wanting to kill more officers, and he continued to fire at the officers who had him trapped in a hallway of the building.

Law enforcement officials felt there was no way they could safely approach Johnson to apprehend him. Brown explained, "We saw no other option but to use our bomb robot. . . . Other options would have exposed our officers to grave danger."[3] Bomb robots such as the one used in the Dallas incident move on specialized wheels or tank-style tracks, and they have arms that can grasp explosive devices. The arm can extend and retract to place the explosive device in a specific location. Dallas police officers operated the bomb robot with a remote control. They used it to carry an explosive near the suspect and then detonate it. This was the first time a robot has been used by US police to kill a suspect. Later, a grand jury investigation concluded that the officers' killing of Johnson was justifiable. The Dallas shooting marked the deadliest single incident for US law enforcement since the terrorist attacks of September 11, 2001, when 72 law enforcement officers died in the line of duty.[4]

People were quick to denounce Johnson's actions in Dallas. This included those protesting police brutality and institutional racism in law enforcement. For example, Black Lives Matter, a movement outspoken on the issue of police brutality against people of color, tweeted, "#BlackLivesMatter advocates dignity, justice and freedom. Not murder."[5]

US LAW ENFORCEMENT TODAY

The Dallas shooting shows how law enforcement officers face the possibility of danger every day in their work. Sometimes officers are the targets and victims of violence. Many people argue that law enforcement officers have the right to use deadly force to protect themselves and their communities from imminent danger.

However, it can be difficult to determine when an imminent threat exists. For example, Officer Jeronimo Yanez, who shot and killed Philando Castile on July 6, 2016, claimed he could not determine whether Castile was reaching for a gun with dangerous intentions. Yanez had stopped Castile's car, and Castile told the officer that he was legally carrying a firearm. But video of the incident showed Castile did not verbally threaten Yanez.[6] Criminal charges were filed against Yanez in connection with the fatal shooting, but the officer was acquitted. However, Yanez was dismissed from his job at the police department after his trial concluded.

A common criticism of law enforcement today questions the use of force, especially deadly force, by officers. Some argue that law enforcement officers use force too often and that officers must be better trained to de-escalate situations.

Furthermore, many argue that police must improve their cultural sensitivity to decrease the high rates of confrontation between people of color and officers.

The events surrounding the Dallas shooting also involve many other concerns and debates regarding law enforcement in the United States today. For instance, the use of a robot to kill Johnson raises questions about how to incorporate new technology into law enforcement in an ethical way. Some believe new technology can help protect law enforcement officers and the communities they serve. Others believe that incorporating certain kinds of technology

Philando Castile was 32 years old when he was fatally shot by a police officer. He worked in nutrition services at Saint Paul Public Schools in Minnesota.

makes law enforcement more like a military organization in a dangerous way. As law enforcement gains new technology, so do criminals, and law enforcement confronts the challenge of evolving to face new threats.

In addition, the Dallas shooting demonstrates the relationship between various law enforcement agencies. According to information released by the US Department of Justice (DOJ) in 2016, there are approximately 18,000 law enforcement agencies in the country, including federal, state, county, and local agencies.[7] Some of those agencies are very large, with more than 30,000 officers, while others

The color blue is traditionally used in memorials for police officers killed in the line of duty.

employ only a single officer. The DOJ reports, "The most common type of agency is the small town police department that employs 10 or fewer officers."[8] At the Dallas shooting, officers from multiple agencies were killed or wounded. This included officers from the DPD, the DART Police, and El Centro College's police department. Additional law enforcement agencies assisted in response to the shooting and during the investigation afterward. Those included the Federal Bureau of Investigation (FBI); the Bureau of Alcohol, Tobacco, Firearms and Explosives (ATF); the US Marshals Service; the Texas Department of Public Safety; and the Texas Rangers, a state law enforcement agency. Each type of agency specializes in specific issues and covers particular jurisdictions.

HISTORICAL ROOTS OF LAW ENFORCEMENT TODAY

Law enforcement has changed a great deal since the early years of the United States. In the 1600s and 1700s, law enforcement was mostly community based and reactive. Local officials, who were often community leaders or unpaid volunteers, typically took action only after a crime occurred rather than taking preemptive measures to deter crime.

An example of reactive policing is arresting someone after a crime is reported. An example of proactive or preventative policing is patrolling an area in the hope that police presence will stop crime before it happens.

Changes in society throughout the 1800s—including growing populations, urbanization, industrialization, and increased immigration—brought about changes in professional law enforcement. Historians note that law enforcement agencies at this time favored the interests of businesses and politicians while unfairly policing certain groups of people, including laborers, low-income people, immigrants, and people of color. This laid the foundations for distrust between law enforcement and members of those groups.

Even seemingly small matters such as police uniforms, which are standard today, have been debated extensively. As official city police departments formed in the 1800s, some encouraged uniforms to make

TO PROTECT AND TO SERVE

In 1963, the Los Angeles Police Department (LAPD) became the first to use the phrase "To Protect and to Serve" as its motto.[9] The LAPD adopted the motto after running a contest in a law enforcement magazine asking for phrases that captured the ideals of the LAPD. The winning entry, submitted by Officer Joseph S. Dorobek, was selected in 1955. The motto became official in 1963 after it was approved by the Los Angeles City Council. The motto is now used by many law enforcement agencies across the country.

officers' presence obvious to the public. They believed this would deter crime and would help people identify officers when they needed them. However, others argued that uniforms were a step toward an unnecessary militarization of law enforcement, and they believed that highlighting the existence of an ever-present police force undermined American ideals of freedom. Still others argued that uniforms would make officers more vulnerable to violence. In the Dallas shooting, uniforms made the officers targets for Johnson, as some had feared when arguing against uniforms two centuries earlier. As US law enforcement encounters new community needs and challenges in the early twenty-first century, historical debates continue to have an impact.

DISCUSSION STARTERS

- How can people express concerns or disagreement with law enforcement policy without violence?
- Does technology such as bomb robots seem to have more benefits or more drawbacks for law enforcement?
- Do you frequently notice law enforcement officers in your community? What kind of officers are they? What job duties are they performing?

CHAPTER TWO

LAW ENFORCEMENT IN EARLY AMERICAN CITIES

Police officers arrest a man in Chicago, Illinois, in the 1890s.

n early America, violent crimes such as murder and robbery were rare. The main safety concerns arose from fires, vagrants, and confrontations between colonists and Native Americans. Instead of from police, enforcement of moral, behavioral, and legal expectations came predominantly from community leaders, especially religious leaders. Judges and jailers also contributed to keeping public order and enforcing laws.

The law enforcement system that did exist followed British practices. It included a system of constables, sheriffs, and citizen watchmen. The first law enforcement officer appointed in the colonies was a constable in Jamestown, in what would later become Virginia, in 1607. The first sheriff is thought to have been appointed in 1634 in the Virginia colony. While colonial governors typically appointed

A colonial judge reads a statement in the 1690s.

sheriffs and constables, some were elected. Constables and sheriffs held many of the same duties, but constables often worked in towns while sheriffs worked in rural areas. Their responsibilities included collecting taxes, serving warrants, bringing suspects and witnesses to court, running jails, and delivering legal documents such as evictions. These duties could be dangerous. The first recorded case of a law enforcement officer being killed in the line of duty was on October 22, 1791, when a sheriff was shot in Columbia County, New York, while delivering a legal document.[1]

Sheriff and constable responsibilities also covered several duties not directly related to law enforcement. These included monitoring health and sanitation conditions and surveying land. Pay for sheriffs and constables was low, and it operated on a fee-based system rather than a regular salary. For example, sheriffs and constables would receive a fee for serving a warrant or collecting a tax. This payment system contributed to the reactionary rather than preventative law enforcement that was typical at the time. Because law enforcement only received payment when following up after illegal activity had already occurred, there was no financial incentive for preventative law enforcement.

In towns, constables were supported by watches composed of citizens who monitored for trouble mostly at night. In the 1630s, Boston, Massachusetts, organized the first night watch. The watchmen's primary responsibilities included reporting fires, monitoring for vagrants, and raising alarm when they detected criminal activity. Over time, watches gained a reputation for being ineffective. Watchmen had less enforcement authority than constables and sheriffs, and their ability to make arrests was limited. Furthermore, common reports of watchmen sleeping and drinking alcohol on duty contributed to the watches' negative reputations.

ESTABLISHING POLICE DEPARTMENTS

Reactionary, community-based policing remained in place into the 1800s. During this century, the country's growth spurred changes to law enforcement structures, leading cities to create official police departments. With these changes came increased rates of crime and social unrest. In the 1830s and 1840s, there were a series of riots provoked by economic turmoil and racial and ethnic tensions.

For example, increased immigration from Ireland brought many workers to Philadelphia, Pennsylvania. These Irish workers competed with the city's low-income

The US Capitol Police (USCP) is one of the oldest law enforcement agencies in the country, dating back to the early 1800s.

white and black communities for jobs. As economic

conditions worsened during a recession in the early

1830s, that competition stiffened, and riots broke out.

The riots destroyed churches, homes, and businesses in

black communities. Violence also targeted Pennsylvania

Hall, a venue constructed to hold lectures, meetings, and

discussions on social and political topics. Just days after

the hall opened in May 1838, a mob of between 200 and

300 young men and boys destroyed the building in a fire.

The mob easily overwhelmed the few constables sent to

guard the building.

The changing demographics in Philadelphia also led to tensions between Irish Catholic immigrants and Protestants born in the United States. The Protestants were known as nativists. Due to immigration, the number of Catholics in the city increased from 35,000 to 170,000 between the years 1830 and 1850.[2] Nativists blamed immigrants for worsening economic problems by working for very low wages, which nativists claimed decreased wages for everyone. Nativists also blamed immigrants for causing competition for housing. There were religious and political differences between the two groups, and nativists faulted immigrants for failing to assimilate. The tensions culminated in a disagreement over how to use different versions of the Bible in schools, which sparked riots in May and July of 1844. These riots caused 20 deaths and injured more than 100 people.[3] The following December, Philadelphia's mayor requested that the state legislature create an official police department "to crush disorder in the bud."[4] Many other cities similarly experienced unrest motivated by tensions in economic class, race, and ethnicity. These tensions continued to develop as city populations grew and changed.

To address these problems, US cities began to adopt a policing model that first started in England in the 1820s.

IRISH AMERICAN POLICE OFFICERS

Irish immigrants were often involved in the violence and rioting that motivated cities to form official police departments, both as instigators and as victims. For much of the 1800s, Irish Americans were negatively stereotyped as dangerous outsiders and criminals. However, as Irish Americans began to represent larger portions of the population, particularly in northeastern cities, they gained some political influence. At a time when law enforcement and politics were intertwined, this influence led to Irish people getting police jobs in exchange for votes and political favors. Additionally, because police salaries were low, the jobs were mostly filled by members of the working class, which included many Irish Americans. In New York City, for example, Irish Americans accounted for more than half of the city's arrests in the 1860s, but they also filled almost half of the city's law enforcement positions. Irish Americans accounted for five of every six officers in the New York City Police Department by the start of the 1900s.[5]

Gaining law enforcement positions validated the sense that Irish immigrants had obtained the rights, freedoms, and protections of other white Americans. Irish Americans believed police work would separate them from other oppressed groups such as black people, who were not regularly employed on police forces in many cities until the second half of the 1900s.

The model emphasized organized and preventative policing. These officers followed regular patrols and wore uniforms. They also had professional hierarchy and discipline similar to that of military forces. Throughout the mid-1800s, cities including Boston; Philadelphia; New York City; Chicago, Illinois; New Orleans, Louisiana; Cincinnati, Ohio; Newark, New Jersey; and Baltimore, Maryland, changed their informal law enforcement systems to official police departments.

But it took some time for city police departments to develop into what they are today. For example, US officers did not initially wear uniforms, and many officers carried department-issued batons rather than firearms. In the second half of the 1800s, city police departments began issuing guns after officers started carrying their own guns while on duty.

Police departments were present in all major American cities by the 1880s. These municipal departments had full-time employees working under a police chief. Taxes and public funding paid employee salaries and supported the departments. Police chiefs were often political appointees who answered to government authorities.

SOCIAL TENSIONS

City police departments were essentially born out of unrest due to social tensions. So, from their beginnings, police were injected into tense situations regarding race, ethnicity, politics, and economic class. Historians observe that police departments in the 1800s typically favored wealthy and powerful people.

To some, this favoritism was evident as police departments worked to break labor strikes after the Civil War (1861–1865). During this time, conflict arose between employers in low-wage industries and their workers. There was increasing unrest among workers over harsh labor conditions that included long hours, dangerous environments, and low pay. The unrest led to strikes,

By the early 1900s, there were several established police departments in the United States.

which slowed productivity for employers and sometimes resulted in violence. Employers often held strong influence over local politics because of their economic power, and city police were typically appointed by politicians. In some cases, officers and police chiefs used political connections or bribes to obtain their positions. This meant employers had significant influence over law enforcement. Meanwhile, working-class and poor people had little or no political influence.

At the same time, city police faced challenges. The political influence over police departments meant staffing was affected by political motivations and election changes. There were high rates of turnover along with minimal training, little professional supervision, and little stability for new police officers. Police officers often faced hostility at work. They also suffered physical attacks. And though deaths were not common, several officers died in the line of duty every year from 1850 onward.[6] Officers were also tasked with monitoring laws that had little public support, such as those regulating gambling, alcohol consumption, and prostitution. Sociology professor Malcolm Holmes and criminal justice professor Brad Smith note that "for their part, citizens frequently challenged police authority, and officers resorted to brutality to establish control."[7]

THE HAYMARKET AFFAIR

In 1886, workers on strike gathered at a rally in Haymarket Square in Chicago to demand an eight-hour workday. At the time, laborers were expected to work long days, sometimes more than 12 hours, for low pay. Police fired guns at the rally in an effort to disperse the crowd. Several strikers were killed or wounded by the gunfire. In response, another rally took place the next day, May 4. As police gave verbal orders to disperse that crowd, someone threw a bomb at the officers. Police responded with gunfire. Several officers and civilians died. The bombing became known as the Haymarket Affair. Historians point out that those responsible for the bomb were a small group of anarchist extremists, not representatives of the labor movement.

IMPLICATIONS FOR THE PRESENT DAY

Many of the issues that developed as law enforcement agencies were formed in the 1800s continue today. For example, people debated how much authority law enforcement could have in relation to American values of freedom and civil liberties. Questions about equipping officers with firearms and requiring them to wear uniforms demonstrated those debates. Furthermore, policing that favored wealthy and powerful people anticipated long-standing concerns about the role of law enforcement in disadvantaged communities. Some believe that the early focus on disadvantaged communities established a law enforcement system that targets people rather than the social and economic conditions that contribute to crime. In the 1800s, those conditions included poverty, unfair working conditions, poor housing, and racial and ethnic tensions. Many of those conditions still exist in some form today, as do instances of law enforcement violence that disproportionately impact communities of color and those who live in poverty.

DISCUSSION STARTERS

- Should all police in the United States carry guns? What are some of the advantages and disadvantages to arming police?
- Is it surprising that the history of law enforcement includes patterns of corruption and mistreatment toward some groups of people?
- How does population growth in cities affect law enforcement needs and the ways law enforcement should work?

CHAPTER THREE

LAW ENFORCEMENT IN EARLY RURAL AMERICA

New Jersey state troopers investigate a wooded area.

As cities across the country established municipal police departments in the 1800s, some differences developed across distinct regions. In the Northeast and Midwest, police departments developed in response to urbanization, labor unrest, and immigration concerns. Other regions also faced these issues, but there were other contributing factors. In the South, the legacy of slave patrols influenced the development of law enforcement. In the West, the challenges of large geographic areas and conflicts between white settlers and Native Americans influenced law enforcement. Some of these historical factors continue to show their effects in interactions between law enforcement and society.

New York City police officers in uniform in 1857

SLAVE PATROLS IN THE SOUTH

The first slave patrols began in South Carolina in the early 1700s. They became more prevalent after the first mass slave uprising in the colonies. The Stono Rebellion of 1739 started in an area near what is now Charleston, South Carolina. It began when a group of approximately 20 slaves broke into a store, killed two white men, and stole guns and ammunition. From there, the group marched south toward Saint Augustine, Florida, a Spanish-controlled area, where they would be free. Dozens of other slaves joined in the march. They killed between 20 and 25 white people along the way. A group of white people pursued the slaves and confronted them in a bloody fight about ten hours after the rebellion started. In total, more than 30 black people died. Another 30 to 40 who managed to escape were later captured. Many of those captured were executed.[1]

In many Southern areas, black slaves outnumbered the white population. White people feared that large uprisings such as the Stono Rebellion would destroy lives and property. As a result, slave patrols took steps to enforce laws and slave codes that limited slave gatherings and activities. For example, in Georgia, slaves could not leave the property

HORRID MASSACRE IN VIRGINIA

Newspapers in the early 1800s used stereotypes to depict slave rebellions.

to which they belonged without written permission.
Slaves also could not travel on main roads in groups of
more than seven without a white person to oversee them.
Additional regulations in many states included curfews and
requirements that slaves carry identification cards. There
were also restrictions on activities that would help slaves
become more independent, such as raising food, earning
money, or learning to read and write. Historian Larry Spruill
notes that laws and slave codes "marked them [slaves] as a
habitual 'dangerous class' requiring relentless supervision
and policing to guarantee their submission."[2] Slave patrols
were in charge of this supervision and policing. The patrols
pursued runaway slaves, punished slaves who broke

plantation rules, employed terror tactics to control slave populations, and enforced each state's laws and slave codes.

Early slave patrols were often informal and voluntary groups who worked without pay or in exchange for small sums of money, alcohol, or tobacco. As the desire for larger and more regular patrols arose, a more formal system developed. In some areas, voluntary participation in slave patrols was expected of all capable white men age 18 to 50. Those who did not participate would sometimes have to pay a fine. In other areas, patrols were made up primarily of white men who were paid on a regular basis. Patrols often walked around towns and cities. In more rural areas, they typically worked in small groups, riding on horseback along a regular route called a beat. These patrols had the authority to carry and use weapons such as guns and whips.

After the Civil War, slave patrols formally disbanded. However, the Ku Klux Klan and other white supremacist groups maintained elements of slave patrol activity such as monitoring black people and committing violent acts. Local police departments also continued to enforce racist practices using laws known as Black Codes in the years following the Civil War, despite efforts by the federal government to prohibit such codes. Similar to slave codes,

Black Codes limited the movements and freedoms of black people through harsh punishment for offenses such as breaking curfew or loitering. Later, law enforcement officials in the South upheld Jim Crow laws, which enforced racial segregation and disenfranchised black people from the late 1800s until the civil rights movement of the 1960s.

THE FIRST BLACK POLICE OFFICERS IN THE SOUTH

The first black police officer in the United States was appointed in Selma, Alabama, in 1867. Subsequent appointments were made soon after in Florida, Texas, and Louisiana. Law professor Stephen L. Carter notes that hiring black officers in Southern cities was a trend after the Civil War "because they were thought to have expertise in how to deal with the formerly enslaved population, and because the existence of black police would keep the freedmen calm."[3] However, black officers were not allowed to arrest white people. That policy continued into the mid-1900s.

The legacy of slave patrols has influenced law enforcement agencies throughout the country. For example, slave patrols helped establish the practice of patrolling a beat, which is still used in American law enforcement today. Some law enforcement officials have also continued slave patrol practices of racial profiling. An officer who is engaging in racial profiling is treating someone as suspect for no reason other than race, whether the officer is aware of it or not. Sometimes this happens when officers stop people who they believe are behaving suspiciously.

LAW ENFORCEMENT IN THE WEST

While cities in the Northeast, Southeast, and Midwest established police departments, many areas of the West did not have big cities with enough people or resources to create such departments. In many Western areas, law enforcement encompassed a mix of local officials, vigilante activity, federal law enforcement, and private investigation agencies.

County sheriffs were often the leading figures of local law enforcement in the West. Sheriffs were typically elected officials who were paid on a fee-based system. They frequently held a wide range of duties, which included serving warrants and subpoenas, overseeing jails, summoning juries and witnesses, executing death warrants, and collecting taxes. Western sheriffs often oversaw large geographic areas. Some counties spread over 800 miles (1,300 km).[4] If sheriffs needed assistance, they had the authority to call capable men in their counties to help. Sheriffs also had the help of constables who oversaw precincts, which were smaller areas within counties. Furthermore, the US Marshals Service, the oldest federal law enforcement agency, helped with the pursuit of notorious fugitives, as did private investigation agencies. As federal officials, US marshals had and continue to have the authority to work across the jurisdictions of individual towns, counties, and states. US marshals still handle fugitive operations today.

NATIVE AMERICAN LAW ENFORCEMENT

Among their various duties, many Western law enforcement units supported the efforts of westward expansion, which included pushing Native Americans out of their own lands and protecting and promoting white settlements. Westward expansion significantly hurt Native American tribes and their systems of justice. As white settlers moved into tribal lands, the federal government signed treaties with Native Americans, preserving portions of territory as Indian country. The federal government assigned white men, called Indian agents, to these areas to oversee US interests. However,

STATE POLICE DEPARTMENTS

State police departments developed later than municipal police departments. The authority of municipal police is restricted to overseeing the laws of particular towns and cities. Throughout the 1800s, challenges arose that showed the limits of local police jurisdictions. State police departments were created to meet these challenges. For instance, state police addressed labor strikes, fugitive pursuits, and other problems that spread beyond local jurisdictions. They also protected wildlife and monitored rural areas. State police became more prominent in the 1900s with the advent of cars and state highway systems, which needed to be patrolled. Today, all states except Hawaii have statewide police departments. Some states call them highway patrols. Hawaii does not have a state police department because of its unique geography as a collection of islands. However, Hawaii, like other states, does have a state department of public safety that coordinates certain law enforcement tasks.

throughout much of the 1800s, Native Americans had the authority to manage wrongdoing among their own people and the tribes within their territories and to administer justice according to their traditions. These traditions often applied restorative justice. For instance, rather than being sent to jail, someone who committed wrongdoing may have been instructed to apologize and provide restitution in the form of supplies or money.

However, the policies of the federal government gradually undermined these traditional methods of justice. The government sponsored tribal police and courts, which implemented practices similar to those of the US criminal justice system. The federal government became more involved in Native American justice systems after a murder on the Great Sioux Reservation in an area that is now South Dakota. The victim, a man named Spotted Tail, and his killer, Crow Dog, were both Brule Sioux. After the murder, the tribe instructed Crow Dog's family to apologize and give Spotted Tail's family money, blankets, and horses. Crow Dog's family complied, and the tribe considered the matter resolved. However, Indian agents condemned the handling of the murder. They argued that harsher punishment was necessary for such a serious crime. The case proceeded to the Supreme

Two Native American police officers on a reservation in South Dakota in the late 1800s

Court, which ruled in 1883 that the federal government did not have authority in crimes between Native Americans.

In response, the US Congress passed the Major Crimes Act in 1885, which increased federal authority over certain crimes, even if both the perpetrator and the victim were Native Americans on tribal territory. These crimes included murder, rape, serious assault, arson, burglary, and larceny. But the act did not give the federal government authority over minor crimes, called misdemeanors. Native Americans still managed misdemeanors that involved only Native Americans on tribal lands. Legal instructor Michael J. Bulzomi explains that law enforcement in Native American territories evolved as "a patchwork of tribal, state, and federal jurisdiction that varies depending on the crime, identity of the perpetrator, identity of the victim, and location of the offense."[5]

Federal and state government intervention in Native American justice systems continued throughout the 1900s and led to confusion over jurisdictional authority, chronic underfunding of Native American law enforcement, and violence between Native Americans and non-Native police. The effects of these problems continue today. Information gathered by the Centers for Disease Control and Prevention from 1999 to 2015 shows that Native Americans experience more fatal police encounters than people of any other racial or ethnic group. The rate of Native Americans being killed by police is 12 percent higher than the rate among black people and 222 percent higher than the rate among white people.[6] Researchers point out that the problem is likely more serious than statistics suggest because law enforcement violence often goes underreported in Native American communities.

DISCUSSION STARTERS

- What similarities and differences stand out about the histories of law enforcement in different parts of the country?
- What are the differences between US justice and law enforcement and traditional Native American justice and law enforcement?
- What stereotypes exist about crime and law enforcement in the "Wild West"? How do those stereotypes compare with the history of law enforcement?

CHAPTER FOUR

FEDERAL LAW ENFORCEMENT

The US Marshals Service is the oldest federal law enforcement agency.

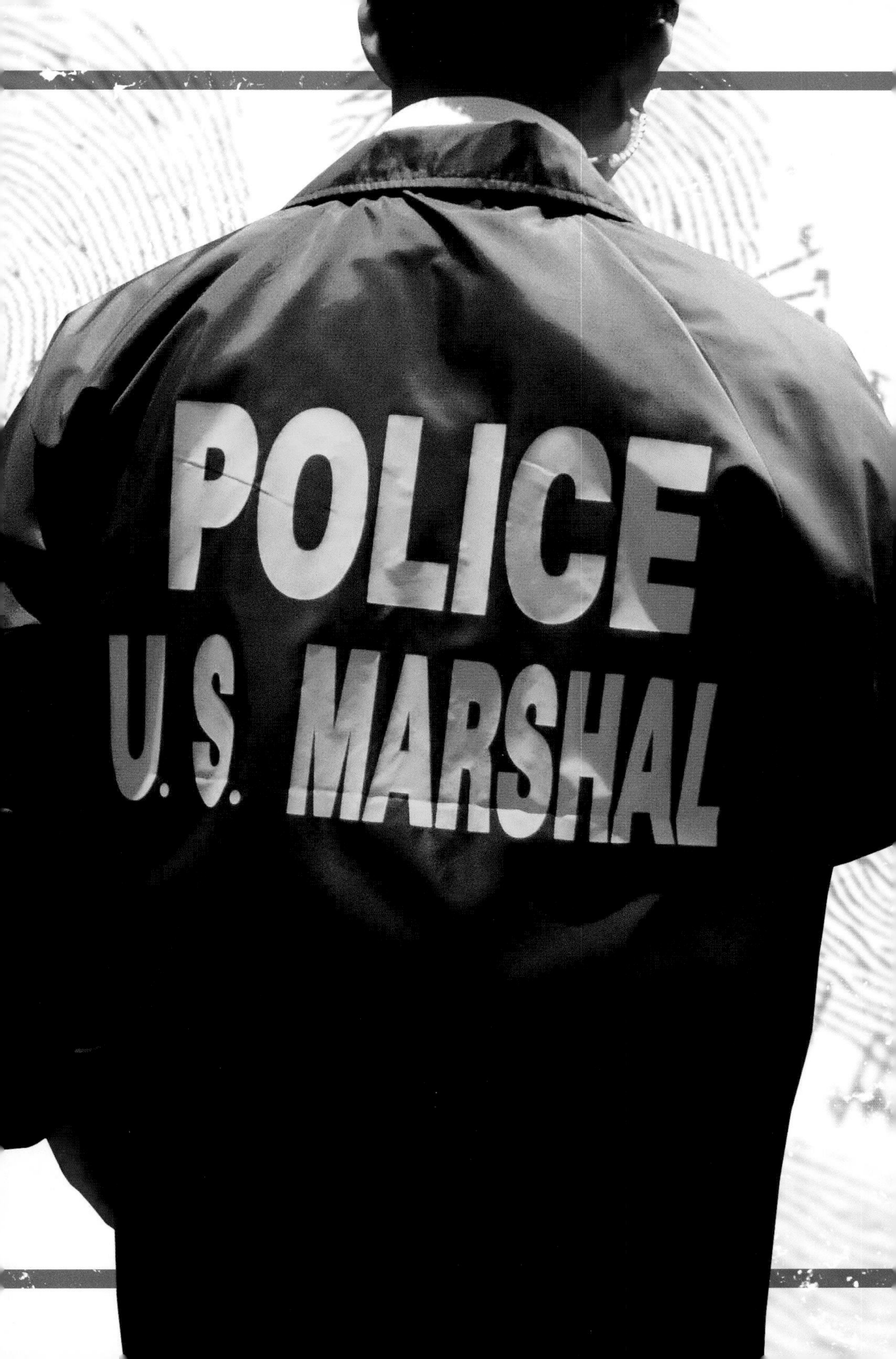
POLICE
U.S. MARSHAL

Whie local law enforcement agencies have jurisdiction in cities and counties, and state agencies enforce statewide laws, federal law enforcement agencies enforce nationwide laws. The first federal law enforcement agency, the US Marshals Service, was created in 1789. Throughout the 1800s, corruption within state and local law enforcement agencies, as well as the increasingly complex problems of the growing country, showed the need for expanded federal agencies. In the early 1900s, the Federal Bureau of Investigation (FBI) formed and played a key role in professionalizing federal law enforcement work.

HISTORY OF FEDERAL LAW ENFORCEMENT

In 1789, President George Washington signed the Judiciary Act, part of which created the US Marshals Service. Washington appointed one marshal to each judicial district. There were 13 marshals in 1789 and 16 by 1791.[1] Their responsibilities included overseeing federal prisoners and executions, conducting the federal census, enforcing federal regulations in areas of westward expansion, monitoring illegal alcohol sales and alcohol tax evasion, combating counterfeiting, and protecting federal judges. Over time, as new federal law enforcement agencies formed, the US

Marshals transferred some of these responsibilities while acquiring new responsibilities. For example, the US Marshals transferred the responsibility for combating counterfeiting to the Secret Service, which formed in 1865 as part of the Department of the Treasury.

The same act that established the US Marshals in 1789 also established the federal position of attorney general to represent the federal government in cases before the US Supreme Court and to advise federal agencies on legal matters. When first created, the Office of the Attorney General employed one person on a part-time basis. That office hired assistants and private attorneys as needed. Eventually, the demands of the position grew so extensive that in 1870, the government decided to create a new executive department called the Department of Justice (DOJ). The Office of the Attorney General led that department. The DOJ also employed

PRESIDENTIAL SECURITY

William McKinley's death was the third presidential assassination in less than 40 years. Abraham Lincoln was shot at a theater in 1865 while the lone police officer assigned to protect him left his post to watch the play. President James Garfield had no security present when he was shot at a train station in Washington, DC, in 1881. When McKinley was shot at a public reception at the Pan American Exposition in Buffalo, New York, he had four Buffalo detectives, four soldiers, and three Secret Service agents in his vicinity.[2] However, protection of the president was still relatively unstructured. After McKinley's death in 1901, the Secret Service developed presidential security into the organized, extensive duty it is today.

assistants to support the attorney general, and it added the Office of Solicitor General, which took over responsibilities for representing the United States in cases before the Supreme Court. Several other agencies, including the US Marshals, came under the authority of the DOJ, and many additional support offices and divisions formed throughout the 1900s. These include the Federal Bureau of Prisons and the Drug Enforcement Administration.

In its early years, the DOJ relied on members of the Secret Service and contracted private investigators to assist with federal investigations. However, Congress banned the government from using private investigators after a violent clash between investigators and striking workers at a steel mill in Pennsylvania killed almost a dozen people in 1892.[3]

A federal Drug Enforcement Administration agent confiscates a bale of cocaine with help from a member of the US Coast Guard.

Then, in 1908, Congress banned the DOJ's use of Secret Service agents. That led the DOJ to form its own investigative and law enforcement body, which would become the FBI.

FORMING THE FBI

The ban on the DOJ's use of Secret Service agents came during President Theodore Roosevelt's efforts to combat corruption in politics, business, and law enforcement. After President William McKinley's assassination in 1901, Roosevelt entered office, bringing experience in law enforcement with him. From 1884 to 1887, Roosevelt served as a deputy sheriff in the Dakota Badlands. From 1895 to 1897, he worked as president of the New York City Police Board, where he gained a reputation for strict adherence to law and order in a time when corruption was widespread. Historian Lewis L. Gould notes, "He went undercover through Manhattan's streets at night to find policemen sleeping on their beats or passing their working hours in saloons."[4] Roosevelt also made it a priority to hire officers based on their qualifications rather than on political favors. He welcomed people of color and the first woman to the city's police headquarters.

Roosevelt's work with the New York City police and his presidential term came at a time when it was common to trade money for political influence and favors. Just before Roosevelt took up his position on the police board, a New York state senate committee had come together to investigate law enforcement corruption in New York City. The committee found widespread problems, including officers interfering in politics, ignoring gambling and prostitution in exchange for bribes, and perpetrating brutality against civilians. People in many cities nationwide worried about law enforcement's inefficiency in addressing problems such as unrest over labor rights, overcrowding and poverty in cities, organized crime, the use of new technology in crime, and anarchism, an anti-authority social and political movement.

FEMALE OFFICERS IN THE NEW YORK CITY POLICE DEPARTMENT

Minnie Gertrude Kelly was the first woman to work in the New York City police headquarters. Roosevelt hired her as a secretary and stenographer. The first woman to work in the city's police force as a detective was Isabella Goodwin, who joined after her husband, a patrolman, died in 1895. Goodwin was promoted to detective after going undercover as a live-in houseworker to solve a major robbery case. The first black woman hired to the force was Cora Parchment, who joined in 1919. Parchment was assigned to welfare work in Harlem.

Throughout the early 1900s, female officers' uniforms were long skirts and high heels. If given service guns, female officers carried the weapons in their purses because their uniforms did not have places to secure a gun. Female officer responsibilities were typically limited to working with youth, female offenders, and sexual assault victims. In the later decades of the 1900s, distinctions between female and male police work began to change. The work gradually became more equal, though there were still cases of discrimination against female officers by male officers and members of the public. Efforts to recruit female officers have improved, but women still make up only a small percentage of the New York City Police Department (NYPD). In 2018, 17 to 18 percent of active officers in the NYPD identified as female while more than 80 percent identified as male.[5]

As president, Roosevelt appointed Charles Bonaparte to the position of attorney general. Bonaparte shared Roosevelt's anti-corruption views. For instance, in one investigation under Bonaparte, the DOJ used Secret Service detectives to examine congressional corruption. This investigation drew criticism from Congress, and it motivated Congress to ban the DOJ's use of Secret Service agents for its investigations. Following the ban, Bonaparte established a new law enforcement body for the DOJ in 1908. It was called the Bureau of Investigation (BOI).

THE EARLY YEARS OF THE FBI

In its early years, the BOI focused primarily on white-collar crimes such as violation of laws regulating business. One of the BOI's first high-profile efforts involved work to enforce the Mann Act of 1910, which targeted prostitution and human trafficking between states. The BOI made hundreds of arrests in enforcement of the Mann Act. Some of those arrests broke up prostitution rings. However, other arrests detained men who were merely traveling between states with women they were not married to. Even though the travel was voluntary, it was illegal according to the wording of the Mann Act. The arrests demonstrated concerns about the negative effects of government overreach in law enforcement. Nevertheless, the BOI's work under the Mann Act drew attention to the organization, and its staff grew from 34 to 360 agents and support personnel by 1915.[6]

During World War I (1914–1918), the BOI assumed responsibility for combating foreign spies and pursuing draft dodgers. Draft dodgers were men who sought to avoid being drafted into the military. During this work, the BOI coordinated with police departments to detain hundreds of thousands of suspected draft dodgers around the country. Most of those arrested were not proven draft dodgers. For instance, of the 125,317 men detained in New York, officials determined that only 1,525 were draft dodgers. There was public outrage over the arrests. Senator Hiram Johnson of California called the BOI's actions "terrorism."[7]

A similar episode occurred after the war when the BOI's attention turned to gathering intelligence on political extremists, anarchists, and communists. After anarchists perpetrated a series of attacks (mostly through mail bombs) on judges, politicians, and business leaders, the BOI began a series of raids. These raids occurred under the leadership of Attorney General A. Mitchell Palmer and DOJ lawyer J. Edgar Hoover. Thousands of people were wrongfully detained in

J. Edgar Hoover was known for investigating activist groups.

what became known as the Palmer Raids.[8] After reports that some of those detained faced unsanitary conditions and police brutality, people protested against the BOI. Though the BOI originated as part of an effort to combat corruption, it was also susceptible to corruption itself.

PROFESSIONALIZING THE FBI IN THE 1930s

In an effort to reform the BOI's image, Attorney General Harlan Fiske Stone appointed Hoover to be the new BOI director in 1924. Hoover would hold the position for 48 years, until his death in 1972. Though Hoover had played a role in some of the BOI's controversial actions, such as the Palmer Raids, he showed commitment to professionalizing the agency. For example, Hoover implemented stricter hiring practices, rigorous training, and stronger management of BOI staff. Hoover also emphasized using science and technology. For instance, just months after Hoover became director, he started the Division of Identification to organize fingerprint collections from US states and other countries. In 1935, Congress changed the BOI's name to the Federal Bureau of Investigation (FBI) after Hoover suggested the need for a more distinctive agency title. In the 1930s, the FBI developed its scientific crime lab. Agents acquired the technology and expert knowledge to assess evidence such as blood samples, handwriting, vehicle tread marks, and ballistics.

As the FBI expanded and professionalized, it also continued to face criticism, especially with regard to the extent of its authority and its relationship to civil rights. For instance, the agency detained more than 110,000 Japanese Americans and placed them in internment camps during World War II (1939–1945).[9] The United States was fighting Japan in the war, but the detainees were Americans and had not committed any crime. These detentions have been widely condemned, both at the time and later, as a violation of individual rights.

Throughout the 1900s, the FBI was criticized for some of the ways it continued to gather information on suspected communists. The agency cooperated with Senator Joseph McCarthy in public hearings that damaged the reputations of many people who proved to have no involvement with radical political activity. The FBI amassed personal information about people's sexual orientation, arguing that government officials in secret gay and lesbian relationships could be vulnerable to blackmail.

Furthermore, some questions focused on the length of time that Hoover spent as FBI director and its implications for unchecked authority. In 1976, Congress set a term limit of ten years, which can be extended by the president only with approval from Congress under special circumstances. Disagreements about constitutional rights, civil liberties, and the extent of federal authority persist in debates about the FBI and its role.

DISCUSSION STARTERS

- What do you think about J. Edgar Hoover's term as FBI director? What positive things did he do for the agency? What negative or corrupt things happened under his watch?
- How do the responsibilities and actions of the FBI compare with those of local police departments?
- What did you know about the FBI before reading its history? How does its history compare with what you know about how the FBI operates today?

CHAPTER FIVE

PROFESSIONALIZING
LOCAL LAW
ENFORCEMENT

Policing techniques changed significantly through the twentieth century due to the professionalism movement.

As federal law enforcement agencies expanded and professionalized to combat corruption in the early 1900s, so did local law enforcement. Before local law enforcement professionalized, officers faced quick turnover and difficult working conditions in their departments. Police officers often had little training. The professionalism movement transformed policing into a long-term career option rooted in education, crime prevention, and science and technology.

EARLY STRATEGIES FOR PROFESSIONALISM

As early as the 1890s, some law enforcement leaders were taking steps toward change. The International Association of Chiefs of Police (IACP) formed in 1893 in the United States. The IACP's goals were to promote high standards of professional behavior, improve international cooperation among law enforcement agencies, improve recruitment and training for new officers, and encourage organized administrations and policies. Only 51 of the 385 invited police chiefs and leaders attended the first IACP meeting, but the organization soon began taking steps to advance its goals.[1] For instance, in 1897, the IACP established the National Bureau of Identification (NBI), a centralized collection of photographs, physical descriptions, and information on criminals. Before the NBI's creation, there was little cooperation between municipal departments to exchange crime data. The NBI became the basis for the FBI's renowned fingerprint collection. The FBI has credited the IACP as the leading organization behind many law enforcement reform efforts in the early 1900s.

One of the most influential leaders to emerge in the professionalism movement was August Vollmer, a police chief in Berkeley, California, who served as IACP president from 1921 to 1922. He gained a reputation as the father of American policing. Vollmer led a number of professionalization initiatives within his department that

The International Association of Chiefs of Police (IACP) remains a leading police organization today. In 2015, President Barack Obama, *right*, spoke at the organization's annual conference.

would later serve as guides for other cities. Those measures included enforcing a code of ethics among his officers and emphasizing education. Vollmer required police officers to obtain a college-level education, which was unusual at the time because many other departments did not even expect officers to have high school diplomas. Vollmer also helped to establish a police training program in 1916 at the University of California, Berkeley—the first of its kind.

August Vollmer in 1929

POLICE COMMUNICATION BEFORE RADIOS

Before radio technology, police departments first used whistles or bells and then turned to signal lights and call boxes to indicate emergencies. Signal lights were developed first. They were red lights placed at central locations, such as a major intersection. When the light was switched on, officers were supposed to check in with the station and respond to a problem. Call boxes were equipped with telegraph technology before the invention of telephones. Officers used call boxes to make regular contact with their stations at required intervals and to send messages requesting help. In Chicago, for example, the telegraphs had a list of situations, including arson, thieves, riot, drunkard, murder, accident, violation of city ordinances, fighting, and fire. Officers simply placed the telegraph's pointer on the situation at hand and pulled a handle to relay an alert to the station. In some places, citizens could also access call boxes to contact police for assistance.

In addition, Vollmer's work highlighted the value of using science and technology in policing. The Berkeley Police Department was the first to become fully mobile in its patrols, initially on bicycles and motorcycles and then in automobiles. The department improved communication through two-way radio technology, and it used polygraph tests, commonly known as lie detector tests. Though polygraph tests have since become controversial, they were initially meant to assist with criminal interrogations as a technological alternative to physical force and other brutal tactics.

Another area of reform focused on officers' working conditions. Vollmer and other leaders believed that better pay and better working conditions were essential to decreasing the underlying causes of corruption and

WALTER GORDON

Walter Gordon joined the Berkeley Police Department in 1919 while he was a student at the University of California, Berkeley, School of Law. He became the first black student to graduate from the program. Gordon worked his patrol at night and took classes during the day. Under the direction of his police chief, August Vollmer, Gordon patrolled the same areas as white officers at a time when black officers were often limited to black neighborhoods. Some Berkeley officers threatened to quit the department if Gordon remained on the force. Vollmer told those officers they could put their badges on the table as they left. Later, Gordon served as a leader in the National Association for the Advancement of Colored People (NAACP). He also served as governor and a federal judge in the US Virgin Islands, positions he was appointed to by President Dwight Eisenhower.

inefficiency within police departments. In departments across the country, officers worked long hours for low pay, infrequent raises, no benefits, and promotions based on an unfair system of political favoritism. For example, in 1919, Boston police officers regularly worked 73 to 98 hours per week.[2] But they earned only $1,400 annually (the equivalent of about $20,917 in 2018).[3] Historians describe the conditions of their police stations as "deplorable."[4] The conditions led more than 1,000 Boston officers to go on strike. The striking officers were fired, and new officers were hired. In contrast, Vollmer's officers received better pay than those in other departments of similar size. Vollmer also enforced fair and equal treatment across racial and gender lines. He was one of the first police chiefs to hire female officers, and he hired Berkeley's first black officer, Walter Gordon.

Vollmer also supported community policing, which was a newly emerging trend. The trend focused on preventing crimes before they occurred and rehabilitating people convicted of crimes. Community policing also questioned crime laws and policies that heavily affected disadvantaged groups of people. For instance, Vollmer questioned police handling of drug investigations and antidrug laws, which disproportionately affected disadvantaged groups. Law professor Charles Wollenberg notes, "[Vollmer] felt police shouldn't be involved in drug law enforcement. He thought drug abuse was a medical issue, a social issue—certainly not a police issue."[5]

Because of Vollmer's initiatives in Berkeley, several other departments—including those in Los Angeles, Chicago, Dallas, and San Diego, California—contracted him to help reorganize their operations. President Herbert Hoover called Vollmer in 1929 to serve alongside other law enforcement leaders on the Wickersham Commission, which studied the state of policing and the widespread problem of police misconduct in the country. As the Wickersham Commission reported, the problems of high crime rates, police corruption, and police brutality persisted, even as the professionalism movement began to emerge. However, historians generally agree that changes initiated by Vollmer and other reformers helped usher in a new era of law enforcement.

IMPROVEMENTS AND CHALLENGES IN THE PROFESSIONALISM MOVEMENT

By the 1950s, departments around the country had adopted the philosophy of professionalism. Many were using strategies outlined in a book by O. W. Wilson called *Police Administration*. Wilson began his career as a patrolman in Vollmer's Berkeley Police Department. He extended the ideas of Vollmer and other leaders in the professionalism movement by focusing on the administrative structure of police departments. This structure adopted a military approach to discipline and organization. It emphasized a central hierarchy of authority, updated and consolidated police facilities, and focused on efficient, preventative crime control. Wilson advocated for close

CARS AND CRIME

Automobiles changed the way police patrolled their communities. They also created new problems and responsibilities for law enforcement. For instance, cars provided fast getaway options for criminals and introduced new crimes such as auto theft. Their growing popularity created new civilian offenses such as jaywalking and parking in prohibited zones. O. W. Wilson observed the impact of cars on crime and on law enforcement's workload. In 1951, he said, "[Cars] have stimulated and facilitated the commission of certain types of crime, and the regulation of their movement and parking is a task, unknown 100 years ago, that today occupies as much as 25 percent of police effort in some communities."[6]

supervision with a chain of command in police departments. He also promoted Vollmer's emphasis on science and technology. In addition to implementing the administrative structure outlined by Wilson, departments also increasingly organized into specialized units that focused on specific law enforcement areas such as traffic, vice, narcotics, juvenile delinquency, and criminal investigation.

Professionalism brought improvements to many departments, but the movement also brought new challenges. The approaches that made law enforcement more bureaucratic, militarily organized, and technological also created distance in the relationship between law enforcement and civilians. For instance, using police cars helped mobilize officers so that they could patrol farther and faster. But car patrols, as opposed to patrol by walking, meant officers talked less with citizens. Furthermore, while preventative policing was meant to decrease crime, the techniques often still targeted minority communities, further increasing tensions between them and law enforcement. For instance, one preventative technique promoted during the professionalism movement was the stop and frisk practice. This practice allows officers to stop people, question them, and pat them down if the officers suspect criminal activity based on their observations. Due to racial profiling, the practice has disproportionately harmed young black men.

The professionalism movement also had a varied effect within police departments. For instance, specialized units gave officers better working hours and let them focus on certain topics to become experts. However, they also divided departments and removed experienced officers from patrol positions to place them in the specialized units. Wilson argued that this could reduce the skill level of patrol units meant to deter crime. The professionalism movement also led officers to unionize. Unions advocated for better officer pay and benefits. They also pushed to decrease the centralized, bureaucratic authority within departments that often silenced officers' input on rules, procedures, and practices. Police unions became a contested political issue, especially in budgetary matters. Unions have also faced criticism for protecting officers accused of brutality.

To summarize the effect of law enforcement changes during the professionalism movement in the first half of the 1900s, criminal justice professor Samuel Walker argues that there were "many achievements in raising the standards of American policing." But he notes there was also "a legacy that rendered American police departments ill-equipped to respond to the multiple crises that engulfed policing in the 1960s."[7] Criminal justice professors Michael D. White and Henry F. Fradella add, "Notably, many of the problems that faced police were tied directly to their inability to connect with citizens, particularly minority citizens."[8] Many reformers such as Vollmer and Wilson wanted to improve community relationships, but those relationships were often lost in reorganizing the scientific, technological, and administrative focuses of departments. The clash between law enforcement and communities of color during the civil rights movement of the 1960s and throughout the later decades of the 1900s demonstrated those problems.

DISCUSSION STARTERS

- In your opinion, which of Vollmer's innovations stand out?
- What impact did technology have on the development of police departments in the early 1900s? What impact does it have on police today?
- History shows that police often faced difficult working conditions. What challenges might police face in their work environments today?

CHAPTER SIX

POLICING AND CIVIL RIGHTS

A police officer wields a club at a black man on the ground during a 1964 riot in north Philadelphia, Pennsylvania.

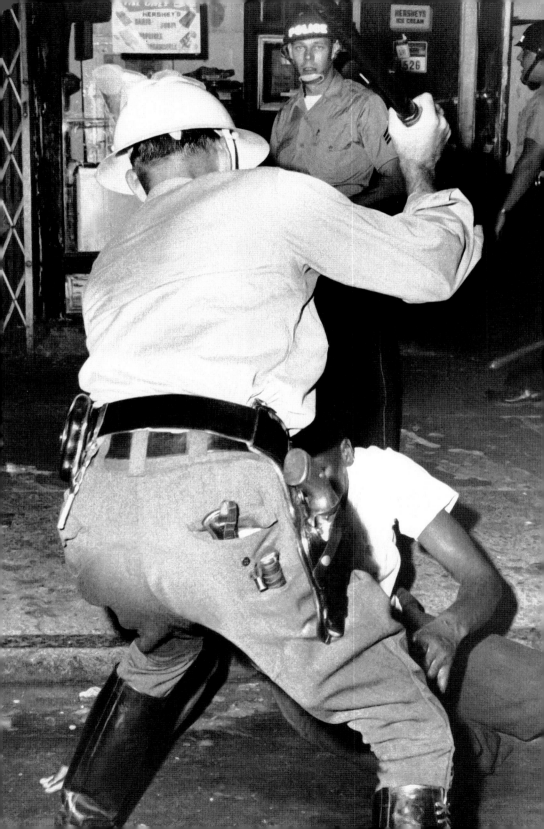

Police brutality has long been associated with race. This association grew from law enforcement's origins in slave patrols and the policing of disadvantaged communities in the 1800s. Even into the 1900s, many white people still considered communities of color to be dangerous. These communities faced higher rates of crime, higher rates of poverty, and higher rates of political disenfranchisement that left them with little power to change this perception or its negative consequences. In the 1960s, civil rights demonstrators who spoke out against the history of police brutality often faced brutality themselves. Martin Luther King Jr. famously included this problem in his August 1963 "I Have a Dream" speech. "We can never be satisfied as long as the Negro is the victim of the unspeakable horrors of police brutality," he said.[1]

BRUTALITY AND RIOTS IN THE 1960s

Many events in the 1960s drew attention to the problems of police brutality that King referenced. For example, during the spring of 1963, just a few months before King's speech, law enforcement displayed extensive use of force in Birmingham, Alabama. Demonstrations against segregation in the city led to thousands of arrests, including 1,000 children and teenagers in early May. Some of the children were as young as six.[2] In addition to making arrests, law enforcement used high-pressure fire hoses, batons, and police dogs on adults and children. A photograph of a 17-year-old boy struggling against a police dog became an iconic image of the brutality.

Alabama and other areas of the South continued to witness police brutality in the years following King's speech. On Bloody Sunday in 1965, for example, law enforcement used violence against approximately 600 civil rights demonstrators who were marching for voting rights.[3] The demonstrators had traveled only six blocks when police used clubs, smoke, nausea gas, and tear gas. Some demonstrators were trampled by police horses. News outlets captured video of the violence and broadcast it across the country. The videos prompted public outcry against police use of force.

Incidents of police brutality against people of color occurred across the country. In New York City, Lieutenant Thomas Gilligan, a white officer, fatally shot James Powell, a black 15-year-old, on July 18, 1964. This sparked the New York Race Riots. In several

K-9 UNITS

Today, K-9 units serve a variety of law enforcement functions. They assist with tracking missing persons and with uncovering drugs or explosives. They can also help to build connections with the community by participating in public programs. Police dogs complete intensive, months-long training with officers.

days of rioting, there was one death, more than 100 injuries, and more than 450 arrests.[4] In August 1965, the Watts Riots in Los Angeles resulted in 34 deaths over six days.[5] The riots began when a fight broke out between police and a crowd of people who had watched a white highway patrolman stop a young black man's car.

The widespread public outcry over police brutality in the 1960s led to some changes aimed at protecting civilians. For example, soon after Bloody Sunday, President Lyndon B. Johnson signed the Voting Rights Act, which outlawed racial discrimination in voting rights, making it easier for people of color to vote. Johnson also created the Kerner Commission in 1967 to address the riots. The commission found that the public's anger was not prompted simply by specific moments of police brutality. The outcry also stemmed from widespread racism that had affected opportunities for communities of color throughout US history. The often-subtle ways this racism had permeated the country's business, education, housing, law enforcement, and other areas is called institutional racism or systemic racism. Institutional racism still affects people in the United States today.

In its report, the Kerner Commission suggested steps to decrease police brutality and rioting in communities of

Four police officers carry a black man suspected of rioting during the New York Race Riots of 1964.

color. This was meant to address what the commission saw as the root causes of police brutality and rioting: poverty and institutional racism. However, the government did not follow many of these suggestions. Instead, government leaders focused on heightened surveillance and combating violent crime. For instance, the Omnibus Crime Control and Safe Streets Act of 1968 contributed to the militarization of state and local law enforcement. Police departments received federal funding to purchase surplus military equipment such as semiautomatic rifles, tanks, bulletproof vests, and walkie-talkies. The act also funded anti-riot squads. These squads developed reputations for disproportionately concentrating on impoverished communities of color. Meanwhile, federal funds offered to pay less than half of the

President Lyndon B. Johnson holds a meeting about the Kerner Commission in 1967.

costs for programs aimed at building relationships between communities and police.

THE WAR ON DRUGS AND MILITARIZATION

Law enforcement militarization continued in the following decades, especially as the federal War on Drugs began. President Richard Nixon initiated the War on Drugs in the 1970s after running a campaign focused on law and order. In the 1980s, President Ronald Reagan focused more law enforcement efforts on combating drugs. The War on Drugs increased punishments for drug crimes. It allowed increased use of stop and frisk, and it permitted state and local law enforcement to use more military equipment.

These law enforcement efforts disproportionately affected communities of color. In 1976, 22 percent of people arrested for drug-related incidents were black. By 1992, that figure had grown to 40 percent, despite the fact that black people made up only about 12 percent of the total population.[6] At the same time, the drug-related arrests of white people had decreased. Jeff Adachi, a public defender in San Francisco, writes, "Countless African Americans suffered lifelong punishment under the drug war's racist enforcement, losing their freedom, their ability to get a job, and even their right to vote."[7] Adachi's point refers to employment practices that prevent people convicted of certain crimes from holding some jobs and to some state laws that prevent convicts and ex-convicts from voting. The War on Drugs faced criticism as a new way to target and disenfranchise black people.

People also criticized law enforcement's militarization and increased use of technology to monitor communities. For example, police created computer databases to track suspected gang members. The Los Angeles Police Department (LAPD) formed an Air Support Division, which used helicopters to watch people without face-to-face interaction. And in one extreme case of militarized policing, officers used an armored vehicle equipped with a battering ram to enter a home where only small amounts of drugs were found. These police actions, which largely focused on people of color, contributed to an oppressive environment.

In 1992, in the context of these changing police strategies, Los Angeles saw its deadliest riots since the 1960s. The riots broke out after four officers on trial for beating Rodney King, a black man, were acquitted in a California state court. The beating occurred after police stopped King for violating his parole. A bystander recorded the encounter on video. The video showed several officers hitting King with batons and kicking him as more than a dozen others watched. The beating reportedly lasted 15 minutes and caused King to suffer skull fractures, permanent brain damage, broken bones, and broken teeth.[8] News media showed the violent video across the country, which provoked outrage. As news of the officers' acquittals emerged, members of black and Latino communities, who had been increasingly subject to police targeting, responded with riots that included fires, looting, and assaults. National Guard and Marine units helped the LAPD respond to the riots. The riots killed dozens of people and injured more than 2,000 others.[9]

THE LEGACY OF POLICE BRUTALITY

After the Los Angeles Riots, there were some changes. Of the four officers who had been acquitted in the California court in relation to beating Rodney King, two were convicted in

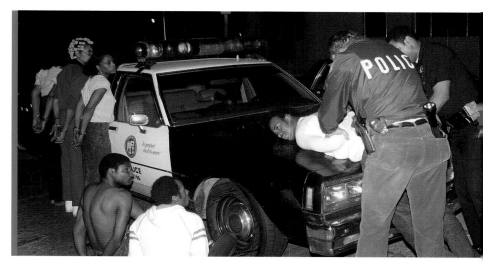

Police handcuff and search a group of people suspected of selling drugs in 1988 in Los Angeles, California.

federal court in 1993 for violating King's civil rights. Neither worked as a police officer again after serving a 30-month prison sentence. The other two officers were fired, and the police chief overseeing them was forced to resign. The community policing movement began to overtake the professionalism movement. Community policing tried to move departments away from the professionalism policies that had distanced officers and civilians. It aimed to address root causes behind strained relationships between law enforcement and civilians. For instance, the Naperville Police Department in Illinois handled a growing gang and burglary problem by opening a neighborhood service center. The center offered crime prevention strategies and relief services, such as helping impoverished people pay their utility bills.

AMBUSH VIOLENCE AGAINST OFFICERS

In 2014, New York City Police Department (NYPD) detectives Rafael Ramos and Wenjian Liu were ambushed and fatally shot by a man named Ismaaiyl Brinsley. The shooting prompted concerns about ambush attacks and revenge violence against law enforcement. Before killing the officers as they sat in their police car, Brinsley expressed anger over the deaths of black men by police. He posted on Instagram, "I'm putting wings on pigs today."[10] The post references a term used by the Black Panthers political group in the 1960s to refer to law enforcement in a derogatory way.

In 2016, both the FBI and the National Law Enforcement Officers Memorial Fund (NLEOMF) reported spikes in officer deaths resulting from ambush attacks. The NLEOMF attributes the rise in part to anti-law enforcement sentiments following high-profile media stories of police brutality. However, the number of officers killed in ambush attacks decreased again in 2017. Researchers note it is too early to determine long-term effects on officer safety since protests against police brutality gained momentum after 2014. Revenge violence has been condemned by mainstream activist movements such as Black Lives Matter.

The motivation behind this approach was to build trust and respect, improve communities, and decrease crime.

However, confrontations between law enforcement and citizens continued. The 2014 response to the police shooting death of unarmed teenager Michael Brown in Ferguson, Missouri, recalled scenes of past violence and militarized policing. The officer who killed Brown, Darren Wilson, claimed that he acted in self-defense. Bystanders recorded video of Brown's body in the street, and violent protests soon began. Police responded to the protests in armored vehicles and riot gear. Wilson was not criminally charged as a result of the shooting. However, a DOJ investigation into the Ferguson Police Department found widespread excessive use of force and racist practices. According to the DOJ, these practices created "deep distrust and hostility often [in] interactions between police and area residents."[11]

In the years after Brown's death, several other high-profile police shootings occurred, many of which were recorded on video and shared on social media and by news outlets. Most police officers in the United States never fire their service weapons or kill civilians. But in recent years, there have been approximately 1,000 fatal police shootings per year in the United States, and many studies indicate that these shootings are underreported.[12] Most of these shootings involve encounters with armed civilians. Those that have sparked protests typically involve unarmed civilians. These deaths bring trauma to communities and serve as reminders that people of color have been unfairly criminalized and targeted by law enforcement throughout history.

DISCUSSION STARTERS

- What is the role of social media in cases of police brutality?
- Has police brutality in the United States changed over the years? If so, has it improved, or has it become worse?
- Do acts of police brutality draw more attention than acts of police bravery and courage? Why or why not?

CHAPTER SEVEN

LAW ENFORCEMENT
AFTER 9/11

In an attack by foreign terrorists, two planes crashed into the two World Trade Center towers in New York City on September 11, 2001.

September 11, 2001, was the deadliest day for law enforcement in US history. Seventy-one officers from various state, local, and federal agencies died responding to the terrorist-attack plane crashes in New York City. One officer died on United Flight 93, which crashed in Shanksville, Pennsylvania. In total, 2,977 people died that day, including civilians, law enforcement and emergency personnel, and members of the military.[1] In the years following the attacks, dozens of other officers died from toxins they were exposed to during rescue and cleanup efforts at Ground Zero, the site where two of the planes crashed into the World Trade Center towers in Manhattan. These deaths highlight the dangerous nature of law enforcement work and the heroic efforts of officers.

The New York City Police Department was one of many law enforcement and emergency response agencies that helped at the scene of the 9/11 attack.

The events of 9/11 also raised questions and new challenges for law enforcement. The extent of the attack prompted departments to reevaluate law enforcement preparedness, strategy, and intelligence capabilities. In response, new law enforcement agencies formed and new policies, procedures, and laws came into effect.

CHANGES IN FEDERAL, STATE, AND LOCAL AGENCIES

After the 9/11 attacks, the federal government passed the USA PATRIOT Act in October 2001, which provided law enforcement officials with more options to track and punish terrorists. Then, in November 2002, the Homeland Security Act passed, creating the US Department of Homeland Security (DHS). DHS began operating in 2003. According to DHS's mission statement, the department oversees "customs,

US FISH & WILDLIFE SERVICE LAW ENFORCEMENT OFFICE

Richard Guadagno was the officer killed on United Flight 93. Guadagno worked for the US Fish & Wildlife Service, which has a law enforcement branch. Federal Wildlife officers ensure the safety of visitors at national wildlife refuges and enforce laws that protect animals and their habitats. Responsibilities may include investigating illegal hunting operations, patrolling for driving violations on refuge land, helping biologists survey the wildlife population, and helping with search-and-rescue operations in the event of accidents or bad weather. These officers can make arrests and carry firearms. Officers go through extensive training, and they take a fitness test because of the job's physical demands.

DEATHS AND INJURIES IN THE LINE OF DUTY

The US Bureau of Labor Statistics reports that law enforcement jobs "can be physically demanding, stressful, and dangerous" and that officers face a greater risk of work-related illness or injury than workers in other fields.[3] In 2014, the rate of work-related deaths for police officers was 13.5 per 100,000 full-time workers. The rate for workers in all other occupations was 3.4 per 100,000. The rate of work-related injuries or illness that required time off was 485.8 per 10,000 full-time officers, compared with 107.1 per 10,000 workers in all other occupations.[4] Injury statistics include accidents (such as falls or car crashes) as well as harm intentionally inflicted by others. However, they do not include assaults against officers that do not result in injury such as spitting, slapping, or kicking. Those kinds of assaults account for the majority of aggression toward police. According to information sent to the FBI, law enforcement agencies reported 60,211 assaults on officers in 2017. Of those, 17,476 (29 percent) resulted in injuries. Law enforcement agencies reported 93 officer deaths to the FBI in 2017. Forty-seven of those deaths were caused by accidents. The remaining 46 were caused by criminal acts.[5]

border, and immigration enforcement, emergency response to natural and manmade disasters, antiterrorism work, and cybersecurity."[2] In an effort to achieve this mission, many changes occurred under DHS, including disbanding some government agencies with law enforcement responsibilities and creating new ones.

Among other changes, DHS replaced the Immigration and Naturalization Service (INS), which had been responsible for monitoring immigration and overseeing the process of becoming a US citizen. In place of INS, DHS established three new agencies under its authority. These include two law enforcement agencies—Customs and Border Protection (CBP) and Immigration and Customs Enforcement (ICE).

THE ABOLISH ICE MOVEMENT

In 2018, political activists began calling for the elimination of ICE. The Abolish ICE movement developed as several ICE practices drew attention under President Donald Trump's administration. For instance, ICE arrests increased more than 40 percent between 2016 and 2017.[6] Information also circulated about undocumented immigrant families being separated along the US-Mexico border. Along with this information came images of children kept in fenced areas away from their parents. Some media outlets, politicians, and activists called these areas cages because of their limited size and metal fencing. These separations were stopped by an executive order from President Trump, but many children remained separated from their families months after the order. Supporters of the Abolish ICE movement argue that the separations and other actions show corruption within ICE that is too widespread and ingrained to reform. Opponents of the movement argue that ICE performs important work in law enforcement and that appropriate changes can be made within the agency. Some of the actions protested in the movement also involve CBP.

The third agency is US Citizenship and Immigration Services (USCIS). CBP monitors the country's borders to protect legal trade and travel and to catch people or materials entering illegally. CBP has the authority to search and question individuals, to detain people for questioning, and to arrest people who are in the country illegally, regardless of whether those people are considered dangerous. While CBP focuses its work at the border, ICE enforces immigration laws within the country and looks for overall security weaknesses.

ICE also has the authority to arrest people who are in the country illegally. CBP and ICE sometimes collaborate in law enforcement efforts. USCIS helps people move through the process of obtaining visas and citizenship.

DHS also oversees the Transportation Security Administration (TSA). TSA formed a year before DHS under the Aviation and Transportation Security Act, which was signed on November 19, 2001. However, as DHS developed, TSA came under its authority. TSA is not a law enforcement agency, but it oversees the Federal Air Marshal Service, which is law enforcement. Federal air marshals travel on flights, armed and undercover, to take action if there is a hijacking, a passenger with an explosive, or another serious threat. TSA also works closely with law enforcement. For example,

A TSA officer pats down a man going through a security checkpoint at Seattle-Tacoma International Airport in Washington.

TSA agents summon airport police if they discover someone carrying a weapon through a security checkpoint.

In addition to prompting changes in federal law enforcement, the 9/11 attacks also brought changes to state and local law enforcement. Before 9/11, counterterrorism was not a focus of state and local law enforcement agencies. However, many of the first responders on scene at the attacks were from state and local agencies. This response prompted state and local law enforcement to consider adding counterterrorism efforts. The LAPD, for example, instituted a new counterterrorism division. One of the division's initiatives was to create a suspicious-activity reporting process to help track and record possible terrorist activity. This has since been used as a model for police nationwide. The LAPD's counterterrorism division also acquired the country's first Hydra system. A Hydra is an elaborate training system of audio material, video material, and staged rooms that simulate emergency situations and terrorism scenarios.

The New York City Police Department (NYPD) also made many changes, including a program that sends detectives to train with police departments in other countries to better understand international threats and safety strategies. Meanwhile, the Louisville Police Department in Kentucky began studying biological warfare such as cases in which people voluntarily infect themselves with dangerous, contagious diseases and then travel to spread the disease. The department partnered with TSA. Other police departments around the country joined in similar steps to address post-9/11 concerns.

Federal, state, and local law enforcement agencies have expanded efforts to work together and streamline communication about threats and preparation. Furthermore, federal programs through DHS and the Department of Defense have expanded militarization of local law enforcement. For example, grants from these programs have helped local police buy military-grade equipment such as drones, armored vehicles, and semiautomatic rifles. This equipment is meant to give officers the capability to respond to an active terrorist attack.

DEBATING THE IMPACT ON CIVIL LIBERTIES

Law enforcement changes after 9/11 were aimed at thwarting terror attacks and preventing catastrophic loss among both law enforcement and civilians. But at the same time, some people have worried about overpolicing and infringements on civil liberties. In particular, people became concerned about privacy amid increased law enforcement presence and surveillance allowed by the USA PATRIOT Act and DHS. And because the terrorists responsible for the 9/11 attacks were Muslim extremists from the Middle East, people also became concerned about racial profiling by law enforcement, especially targeting Middle Eastern and Asian communities, even though it is illegal.

Criminologist Yarin Eski observes that increased law enforcement presence, surveillance, and racial profiling became evident in many public places such as malls, train stations, and airports after the changes ushered in by

A crowd protests in November 2011, asking for Muslims to be treated fairly. The religious group and people who are perceived as Muslim have faced increased discrimination since 9/11.

the USA PATRIOT Act and DHS. Eski writes that travelers encounter "barricades, border control, anti-terrorist units, (armed) police, customs forces and security officers . . . demanding identification and enforcing their far-reaching powers on 'randomly' selected individuals whose carry-on luggage as well as themselves are thoroughly inspected."[7] Eski emphasizes the word *randomly* because research shows that counterterrorism law enforcement practices have disproportionately targeted Muslims and Arab Americans. For example, Peter Siggins, who worked as chief deputy attorney general in California, notes that federal officials contacted more than 200 colleges and universities to collect information about Middle Eastern students in the months following 9/11.

In response to these concerns about overpolicing, some police departments have created new opportunities for community involvement. They argue that such involvement can help with security efforts and build trust between law enforcement and communities. For example, in Dearborn, Michigan, where there is a large Arab and Muslim population, the local police department has worked to encourage members of the community to see themselves as partners in law enforcement. Dearborn began a program called Building

Respect in Diverse Groups to Enhance Ethnic Sensitivity (BRIDGES), a partnership among Arab American groups, state and local police, the FBI, and other community members. After 9/11, BRIDGES began holding meetings where people could voice concerns and ideas for solutions. These ideas brought change. For example, the improved trust between law enforcement and the community led to a civilian report that helped law enforcement stop a planned shooting attack at Wayne State University's Medical School. A group of Arab American students called police to report the suspected shooter, a former medical student, after they saw him in a park wearing dark clothing and holding a firearm. Dearborn's mayor, John O'Reilly, believes the students were not afraid to contact police because of efforts to demonstrate that police are not enemies of the Arab American community. Other cities have since followed Dearborn's BRIDGES model.

DISCUSSION STARTERS

- What is the best way to balance national security against individual rights such as the right to privacy?
- Do local police departments need military-grade equipment?
- What should police departments do to decrease racial profiling?

CHAPTER EIGHT

LAW ENFORCEMENT TODAY AND IN THE FUTURE

New technologies, including tablets, have changed police work.

I n a speech at a memorial service for the five officers killed in the 2016 Dallas shooting, President Barack Obama said, "We ask the police to do too much and we ask too little of ourselves." He explained, "We tell the police 'you're a social worker, you're the parent, you're the teacher, you're the drug counselor.' We tell them to keep those neighborhoods in check at all costs, and do so without causing any political blowback or inconvenience. . . . And then we feign surprise when, periodically, the tensions boil over."[1] The Dallas police chief at the time, David Brown, expressed similar thoughts, as have other enforcement officials.

Today, law enforcement faces a variety of complex challenges. These include increases in mass shootings, cybercrimes, and threats of international and domestic terrorism, in addition to the regular work of maintaining

President Barack Obama hugs Dallas police chief David Brown at a memorial service days after the 2016 shooting attack against police in Dallas.

safety in communities through tasks such as traffic patrol and criminal investigations. Another major challenge for law enforcement is moving beyond historical legacies of corruption and violence within certain communities. Amid these challenges, police departments deal with tight budgets and struggle to recruit officers. This range of expectations and demands has prompted some to question whether government and society expect too much of police today, especially as law enforcement faces heightened scrutiny and negativity. As government, law enforcement, and society consider this question, they also consider the role of law enforcement in the future and ways to decrease the burden that some feel has been placed on law enforcement.

EDUCATION AND MENTAL HEALTH

According to the National Association of School Resource Officers (NASRO), "School-based policing is the fastest-growing area of law enforcement."[2]

DIVERSITY IN LAW ENFORCEMENT

In 2013, a survey sponsored by the US Bureau of Justice Statistics found that "about 27% of local police officers were members of a racial or ethnic minority, compared to 15% in 1987." About 12 percent of local police officers were women, which had increased from 8 percent in 1987.[3] Still, these percentages are not representative of the population as a whole. Approximately 40 percent of the US population are people of color, and just over one-half of the population are women.[4]

POLICE TECHNOLOGY
IN THE TWENTY-FIRST CENTURY

Throughout its history, law enforcement has implemented new technology in its operations, and departments and agencies continue to incorporate advancements. For example, following instances of police brutality that began drawing increased attention in 2014, more police started wearing body cameras to record their activity. These recordings are meant to protect the safety and accountability of both officers and the public. Recently, law enforcement has also employed drones to follow stolen cars and to track criminals.

New technologies are also being used to find out when and where crime happens. More than 85 cities use a system called ShotSpotter, which uses sensors to detect gunfire and send immediate alerts to law enforcement.[5] The alerts include specific information such as the location of the shots and the amount and type of gunfire. Throughout 2018, police in Louisville, Kentucky, worked to become the first to link ShotSpotter and drones. The proposed link would automatically send a drone to a location as soon as ShotSpotter issues an alert. The drone would relay the

Fresno, California, police chief Jerry Dyer shows a screen depicting results of ShotSpotter gunshot detection technology.

visual scene to law enforcement to help them prepare their plan from a safe location.

Law enforcement agencies in some areas also use drones and fixed surveillance cameras to monitor areas. These systems are equipped with software that analyzes the surveillance feeds in real time to produce information about crime patterns. These systems can also operate with facial recognition software, which would allow them to use their systems of cameras and drones to locate suspects. For instance, officers could upload an image of the suspect, and the surveillance system would scan crowds and passersby looking for a match. While presenting advanced options for efficiency and safety, new technology has raised concerns about privacy, civil liberties, and profiling that police continue to consider.

NASRO reports that there are an estimated 14,000 to 20,000 resource officers in US schools.[6] Many view these officers as a necessary protection against school shootings and other violent disturbances. But some argue that it is less important to increase law enforcement presence and more important to focus on education, social work, and mental health to decrease crime and violence. They argue that many problems the law enforcement community encounters are really problems that should be addressed by other professions.

In the case of schools, for example, educators and law enforcement have considered ways to involve police less frequently and more efficiently. For instance, at a middle school in Green Bay, Wisconsin, school resource officers had been responding to minor problems such as dress

LEARNING HOW TO INTERACT WITH POLICE

In 2017 and 2018, New Jersey considered a bill that would require school lessons on interacting with police. The lessons would be part of the statewide social studies curriculum from kindergarten through grade 12. Schools would receive input from police groups, legal experts, and educators to develop lessons. Many of these groups have already been conducting presentations about police and community interactions for years, but these recent legislative initiatives are a new trend. Other states have introduced similar legislation, and some have added these kinds of lessons in driver's education courses.

Proponents of these lessons say they aim to keep both officers and young people safe during encounters and to inform students of their rights. For example, students learn that if they believe they have been unfairly stopped for a traffic violation, the place to fight the ticket is in court, not in a combative way with the officer on the street. Opponents argue that these programs place too much responsibility and accountability on young people instead of on law enforcement.

code violations. Those situations could escalate and result in a ticket for the student. The school noticed persistent problems with vandalism, students carrying weapons, and students assaulting other students and teachers. To address these problems, the school reevaluated its reliance on law enforcement and added more staff including an associate principal and a school counselor. Administrators now handle more discipline issues such as dress code violations, and they coordinate with students, families, and school resource officers to address larger problems.

Mental health is another issue that arises frequently in discussions of law enforcement workloads. Many calls to law enforcement involve a person with mental illness. For example, in 2015, the NYPD responded to 300 cases per day involving what they referred to as people with emotional disturbances.[7] A 2013 report from police in Tucson, Arizona, revealed "more calls about mental illness than about burglaries or stolen cars."[8]

Booker Hodges, who works as an undersheriff and a crisis intervention team (CIT) coach in Saint Paul, Minnesota, argues that police are not necessarily the best responders for incidents of mental illness, especially nonviolent incidents. Hodges notes that psychologists and other mental health professionals study for seven to 12 years of higher education and receive supervised training for hundreds of hours. On the other hand, police officers may receive 40 hours of training in a CIT course with a mental health component. Because of this difference, Hodges believes "we are setting police officers up for failure by continuing to send them on calls that, in spite of our best efforts, we can never train them well enough to handle."[9] Without proper training, encounters between law enforcement and people with mental illness can become dangerous or deadly. People with mental illness are more likely to be killed by police than those without mental illness. While officers emphasize that building awareness of mental illness is important to their jobs, they also stress that other professionals have more appropriate skills to address the issue.

MENTAL HEALTH AMONG POLICE

Andy O'Hara worked for the California Highway Patrol and then founded Badge of Life, a nonprofit mental health education organization. He and his research colleagues note, "Police officers are more likely to die by suicide than by any type of criminal or criminal activity."[10] Law enforcement work is stressful, dangerous, traumatic, and at times boring or monotonous. It often involves long shifts and challenges to work-life balance. These conditions may strain officers' emotional well-being and mental health. Furthermore, law enforcement officers have identified a lack of resources and a culture of silence within departments that makes it challenging to report mental health concerns. Officers worry that they may be seen as weak, unfit for duty, or poor candidates for promotions if they disclose mental health concerns. Advocates such as O'Hara have worked to change that culture.

Hodges suggests one idea to help solve the problem: investing in teams of mental health professionals and social workers who can respond to situations 24 hours a day, seven days a week, just as police would. Another suggestion is to have specialized police units for calls related to mental health. In addition, some argue that there should be better access to mental health resources in educational and medical settings to treat conditions before a crisis occurs. These kinds of suggestions that depend less on law enforcement and more on social services have been considered for other problems as well, such as addiction, poverty, and chronic homelessness. For instance, Seattle, Washington, implemented its law enforcement assisted diversion (LEAD) program in 2011. The program helps officers send people who have committed low-level crimes to case managers

As part of the Seattle Police Department's LEAD program, an officer talks with a woman sitting outside.

rather than bring them into the criminal justice system. The case managers create tailored plans "focused on improving quality of life and reducing criminal behavior. In many cases, clients are seeking food, housing, job opportunities or treatment for drug addiction."[11] The program has helped reduce the likelihood that people will repeat offenses, which means fewer encounters with law enforcement.

HOW TO BECOME A POLICE OFFICER

Requirements for becoming a police officer vary by department, but some general guidelines apply to most departments. People interested in becoming police officers usually complete higher education courses through a community college, university, or police academy. These cover information about laws and the criminal justice system. The application process generally includes a written test, interviews, background checks, physical fitness tests, psychological screenings, polygraph tests, drug screenings, and questionnaires about finances, employment history, and personal life. Applicants must be US citizens, have a valid driver's license, have no felony convictions, and be 21 years old by the time they finish training.

LOOKING AHEAD

Law enforcement has changed significantly since the early days of the United States. No longer made up of informal watches and patrols, law enforcement now consists of full-time, professional departments and agencies that serve the needs of cities, states, and the nation. Many consider law enforcement to be a long-term career and a calling, and officers often express pride in protecting and serving their communities. As law enforcement looks to the future and its needs, officers also acknowledge ongoing challenges. Terrence Cunningham, a leader in the International Association of Chiefs of Police, addressed issues of the past, present, and future in remarks at a conference in 2016. Cunningham said, "Over the years, thousands of police officers have laid down their lives for their fellow citizens while hundreds of thousands more have been injured." But, he acknowledged, "the history of policing has also had darker periods." Cunningham apologized for those darker periods while also noting that current and future officers "are not to blame" for injustices they did not commit. He concluded, "All members of our society must realize that we have a mutual obligation to work together to ensure fairness, dignity, security, and justice."[12]

DISCUSSION STARTERS

- Are law enforcement officers, especially local police, expected to do too much in the course of their jobs?
- What new kinds of problems or crimes might law enforcement face in the next 50, 100, or 200 years?
- How can citizens and members of other professions assist with the problems law enforcement officers encounter?

ESSENTIAL FACTS

SIGNIFICANT EVENTS

- On April 29, 1992, riots broke out in Los Angeles following the acquittal of four police officers. They were on trial for beating Rodney King, a black man, as other officers watched. News media had publicized a video of King's beating obtained from a bystander.

- On September 11, 2001, law enforcement suffered its deadliest day in US history. Seventy-two officers died in the terrorist attacks on that day. In the years following the attacks, many other officers have died from exposure to toxins during rescue and cleanup efforts. The 9/11 attacks led to widespread changes in law enforcement.

- On August 9, 2014, Officer Darren Wilson shot and killed Michael Brown, an unarmed black teenager, in Ferguson, Missouri. The shooting sparked protests and fueled national attention to several subsequent instances of police brutality against people of color.

KEY PLAYERS

- President Theodore Roosevelt helped form an agency now known as the Federal Bureau of Investigation (FBI).

- August Vollmer, a police chief in Berkeley, California, emerged as a leader in the law enforcement professionalism movement, emphasizing education, technological innovation, and ethics.

- J. Edgar Hoover was director of the FBI from 1924 to 1972, during which time he professionalized the agency and developed its scientific crime lab.

- David Brown, a black man and the Dallas police chief during an ambush killing in 2016, emerged as a leader against revenge killings of police and an advocate for fair workloads and working conditions for police.

IMPACT ON SOCIETY

Society depends on law enforcement to provide safety, to maintain order, and to offer expert assistance in times of emergency and trouble. Law enforcement in the United States has developed from informal community watches and patrols in the 1600s and 1700s to an extensive network of approximately 18,000 official agencies. These agencies serve communities at the federal, state, county, and local levels. Their budgets come from public funding. Law enforcement has historically abused its authority by oppressing marginalized communities, including immigrants, low-wage workers, people living in poverty, and people of color. This legacy continues to affect law enforcement relations with these communities today. When police use force viewed as excessive or abusive, it brings trauma to individuals and communities. Law enforcement methods also raise questions about the balance between public security and personal freedoms. Reformers both inside and outside law enforcement have sought to make policing fairer and more equitable.

QUOTE

"We ask the police to do too much and we ask too little of ourselves. We tell the police 'you're a social worker, you're the parent, you're the teacher, you're the drug counselor.' We tell them to keep those neighborhoods in check at all costs, and do so without causing any political blowback or inconvenience. . . . And then we feign surprise when, periodically, the tensions boil over."

—President Barack Obama, speaking at a memorial for fallen Dallas police officers in 2016

GLOSSARY

acquitted
Found not guilty of a criminal act.

beat
A route regularly patrolled by a law enforcement officer.

brutality
Cruel, harsh, and violent treatment of another person.

bureaucratic
Concerned with the administrative work of managing an agency, usually viewed as complex and impersonal.

counterfeiting
Making a fake copy of an item, usually money.

counterterrorism
Strategies to prevent terrorism.

disenfranchise
To take away voting rights.

grand jury
A group of citizens tasked with examining accusations to determine whether criminal charges should be filed.

hierarchy
A clear chain of command from the most authoritative individual to the least.

jurisdiction
A certain area within which a group has authority to make a legal decision or take legal action.

militarized
When an object, person, group, or concept takes on military qualities.

municipal
Related to a city or town or to local government.

parole
Early release from prison because of good behavior under the condition that good behavior continue.

preventative
Having to do with stopping a problem before it arises.

professionalism movement
An approach to law enforcement that focused on strong departmental organization, clear authority, use of technology, and long-term careers.

racial profiling
Using racial characteristics to determine whether a person may be committing an illegal activity.

reactive
Having to do with taking action after a problem arises.

restorative justice
A system that allows wrongdoers to atone for their actions and reenter society.

strike
A workers' protest that involves refusing to work until requests are met.

subpoena
An official written command that summons a person to appear in court.

vagrant
A homeless person who does not typically remain in the same city or state for much time.

ADDITIONAL RESOURCES

SELECTED BIBLIOGRAPHY

Flamm, Michael W. *In the Heat of the Summer: The New York Riots of 1964 and the War on Crime*. U of Pennsylvania P, 2017.

Jeffreys-Jones, Rhodri. *The FBI: A History*. Yale UP, 2007.

Leo, Richard A. *Police Interrogation and American Justice*. Harvard UP, 2008.

Potter, Gary. "The History of Policing in the United States." *Police Studies Online*. Eastern Kentucky University, 25 June 2013. plsonline.eku.edu. Accessed 10 Aug. 2018.

FURTHER READINGS

Harris, Duchess, and Rebecca Morris. *The Right to Bear Arms*. Abdo, 2018.

Harris, Duchess, and Rebecca Rissman. *Race and Policing*. Abdo, 2018.

Mullenbach, Cheryl. *Women in Blue: 16 Brave Officers, Forensics Experts, Police Chiefs, and More*. Chicago Review, 2016.

ONLINE RESOURCES

To learn more about the history of law enforcement, visit **abdobooklinks.com** or scan this QR code. These links are routinely monitored and updated to provide the most current information available.

MORE INFORMATION

For more information on this subject, contact or visit the following organizations:

Fraternal Order of Police

701 Marriott Dr.
Nashville, TN 37214
615-399-0900
fop.net

The Fraternal Order of Police is the largest law enforcement organization in the world. It develops educational programs, hosts social gatherings, and organizes charity events to assist police officers and the community through such services as underage-drinking prevention programs, veterans' assistance, and support plans for law enforcement families.

National Law Enforcement Museum

444 E St. NW
Washington, DC 20001
202-737-3400
lawenforcementmuseum.org

The National Law Enforcement Museum contains exhibits on the history of policing. The museum runs workshops for students of all ages and adults, offers guided tours, and provides immersion experiences that allow visitors to walk through the daily work of law enforcement.

National Organization of Black Law Enforcement Executives (NOBLE)

4609-F Pinecrest Office Park Dr.
Alexandria, VA 22312-1442
703-658-1529
noblenational.org

NOBLE is an organization of leaders from federal, state, and local agencies. NOBLE runs community programs, has mentoring programs for officers of color, conducts research, and leads collaborative reform initiatives.

SOURCE NOTES

CHAPTER 1. A SHOOTING ATTACK IN DALLAS

1. Tessa Berenson and Katie Reilly. "Everything We Know So Far about the Dallas Shooting Suspect." *Time*, 8 July 2016, time.com. Accessed 10 Jan. 2019.

2. Molly Hennessy-Fiske. "She Wasn't a Cop and She Wasn't White, but She Took a Bullet in Dallas While Protecting Her Sons." *Los Angeles Times*, 10 July 2016, latimes.com. Accessed 10 Jan. 2019.

3. Berenson and Reilly, "Everything We Know So Far about the Dallas Shooting Suspect."

4. Kim Soffen. "The Dallas Sniper Attack Was the Deadliest Event for Police since 9/11." *Washington Post*, 8 July 2016, washingtonpost.com. Accessed 10 Jan. 2019.

5. "Black Lives Matter Decries Dallas Shooting." *Reuters*, 8 July 2016, reuters.com. Accessed 10 Jan. 2019.

6. "Women Streams Graphic Video of Boyfriend Shot by Police." *CNN*, n.d., cnn.com. Accessed 10 Jan. 2019.

7. Duren Banks et al. "National Sources of Law Enforcement Employment Data." *US Department of Justice, Office of Justice Programs, Bureau of Justice Statistics*, 4 Oct. 2016, bjs.gov. Accessed 10 Jan. 2019.

8. Banks et al., "National Sources of Law Enforcement Employment Data."

9. "The Origin of the LAPD Motto." *Los Angeles Police Department*, 2018, lapdonline.org. Accessed 10 Jan. 2019. Originally published in *BEAT*, December 1963.

CHAPTER 2. LAW ENFORCEMENT IN EARLY AMERICAN CITIES

1. National Law Enforcement Officers Memorial Fund. "The Early Days of American Law Enforcement." *Fed Agent*, 12 Apr. 2012, fedagent.com. Accessed 10 Jan. 2019.

2. Sandy Hingston. "Bullets and Bigots: Remembering Philadelphia's 1844 Anti-Catholic Riots." *Philadelphia Magazine*, 17 Dec. 2015, phillymag.com. Accessed 10 Jan. 2019.

3. Melissa Mandell. "The Kingston Riots of 1844." *PhilaPlace*, n.d., philaplace.org. Accessed 10 Jan. 2019.

4. Alasdair Roberts. *The End of Protest: How Free-Market Capitalism Learned to Control Dissent.* Cornell UP, 2013. 20. *Google Books*. Accessed 10 Jan. 2019.

5. Patrick O'Brien. "Irish Americans." *The Social History of Crime and Punishment in America: An Encyclopedia*, edited by Wilbur R. Miller, Sage, 2012. 861. *Amazon*. Accessed 10 Jan. 2019.

6. "Year-by-Year Breakdown of Law Enforcement Deaths throughout US History." *National Law Enforcement Officers Memorial Fund*, 16 Mar. 2018, nleomf.org. Accessed 10 Jan. 2019.

7. Malcolm D. Holmes and Brad W. Smith. *Race and Police Brutality: Roots of an Urban Dilemma.* State U of New York P, 2008. 23. *Google Books*. Accessed 10 Jan. 2019.

CHAPTER 3. LAW ENFORCEMENT IN EARLY RURAL AMERICA

1. "Slave Rebellions." *National Park Service*, 6 Sept. 2011, nps.gov. Accessed 10 Jan. 2019.

2. Larry H. Spruill. "Slave Patrols, 'Packs of Negro Dogs' and Policing Black Communities." *Phylon*, vol. 53, no. 1, Summer 2016, 50. *JSTOR*. Accessed 10 Jan. 2019.

3. Stephen L. Carter. "Policing and Oppression Have a Long History." *Bloomberg*, 29 Oct. 2015, bloomberg.com. Accessed 10 Jan. 2019.

4. Larry D. Ball. *Desert Lawmen: The High Sheriffs of New Mexico and Arizona 1846–1912*. U of New Mexico P, 1992. 10–11. *Google Books*. Accessed 10 Jan. 2019.

5. Michael J. Bulzomi. "Indian Country and the Tribal Law and Order Act of 2010." *FBI Law Enforcement Bulletin*, 1 May 2012, leb.fbi.gov. Accessed 10 Jan. 2019.

6. Eliza Racine. "Native Lives Matter: The Overlooked Police Brutality against Native Americans." *Lakota People's Law Project*, 21 Nov. 2017, lakotalaw.org. Accessed 10 Jan. 2019.

CHAPTER 4. FEDERAL LAW ENFORCEMENT

1. "History—The First Generation of United States Marshals." *US Marshals Service*, n.d., usmarshals.gov. Accessed 10 Jan. 2019.

2. "JFK Assassination Records: Appendix 7; A Brief History of Presidential Protection." *National Archives*, 15 Aug. 2016, archives.gov. Accessed 10 Jan. 2019.

3. "The Strike at Homestead Mill." *PBS: American Experience*, n.d., pbs.org. Accessed 10 Jan. 2019.

4. Lewis L. Gould. *Theodore Roosevelt*. Oxford UP, 2012. 17. *Google Books*. Accessed 10 Jan. 2019.

5. "Current NYPD Members of Service." *Civilian Complaint Review Board, Data Transparency Initiative*, 2018, nyc.gov. Accessed 10 Jan. 2019.

6. "The Nation Calls, 1908–1923." *Federal Bureau of Investigation*, n.d., fbi.gov. Accessed 10 Jan. 2019.

7. Michael Newton. *The FBI and the KKK: A Critical History*. McFarland, 2005. 16. *Google Books*. Accessed 10 Jan. 2019.

8. "Palmer Raids." *Federal Bureau of Investigation*, n.d., fbi.gov. Accessed 10 Jan. 2019.

9. T. A. Frail. "The Injustice of Japanese-American Internment Camps Resonates Strongly to This Day." *Smithsonian*, Jan. 2017, smithsonianmag.com. Accessed 10 Jan. 2019.

CHAPTER 5. PROFESSIONALIZING LOCAL LAW ENFORCEMENT

1. James W. Sterling. "A History of the IACP Insignia." *Police Chief,* n.d., policechiefmagazine.org. Accessed 10 Jan. 2019.

2. Catherine Fisk and L Song Richardson. "Police Unions." *George Washington Law Review*, vol. 85, no. 3, May 2017, 734. *Berkeley Law Scholarship Repository*, scholarship.law.berkeley.edu. Accessed 10 Jan. 2019.

3. David H. McElreath et al. *Introduction to Law Enforcement*. CRC, 2013. 50. *Google Books*. Accessed 10 Jan. 2019.

4. Brian Farmer. "The Boston Police Strike of 1919." *New American*, 15 July 2011, thenewamerican.com. Accessed 10 Jan. 2019.

5. Glen Martin. "Black Cop, White Cop: What Can Two Berkeley Police from the Century Before Tell Us about Race Relations in America Today?" *California*, Fall 2015, alumni.berkeley.edu. Accessed 10 Jan. 2019.

6. O. W. Wilson. "Progress in Police Administration." *Journal of Criminal Law and Criminology*, vol. 42, issue 2, Summer 1951, 142. *Northwestern University School of Law Scholarly Commons*, scholarlycommons.law.northwestern.edu. Accessed 10 Jan. 2019.

SOURCE NOTES CONTINUED

7. Samuel Walker. "Governing the American Police: Wrestling with the Problems of Democracy." *University of Chicago Legal Forum*, vol. 2016, article 15, 2016, 630–631. *Chicago Unbound*, chicagounbound.uchicago.edu. Accessed 10 Jan. 2019.

8. Michael D. White and Henry F. Fradella. *Stop and Frisk: The Use and Abuse of a Controversial Policing Tactic*. New York UP, 2016. 153. *Google Books*. Accessed 10 Jan. 2019.

CHAPTER 6. POLICING AND CIVIL RIGHTS

1. Martin Luther King Jr. "I Have a Dream…" *National Archives*, 1963, archives.gov. Accessed 10 Jan. 2019.

2. "Alabama: West Park Birmingham." *National Park Service*, 28 July 2017, nps.gov. Accessed 10 Jan. 2019.

3. "Bloody Sunday." *National Park Service: Selma to Montgomery National Historical Trail Alabama*, 9 Aug. 2018, nps.gov. Accessed 10 Jan. 2019.

4. "New York Race Riots." *Civil Rights Digital Library*, 2013, crdl.usg.edu. Accessed 10 Jan. 2019.

5. "Watts Riots." *History*, 21 Aug. 2018, history.com. Accessed 10 Jan. 2019.

6. Hannah LF Cooper. "War on Drugs Policing and Police Brutality." *Substance Use & Misuse*, vol. 50, issue 8–9, 2015. Author manuscript. *PubMed Central*, ncbi.nlm.nih.gov. Accessed 10 Jan. 2019.

7. Jeff Adachi. "Police Militarization and the War on Citizens." *Human Rights Magazine*, vol. 42, no. 1, 2017, americanbar.org. Accessed 25 Nov. 2018.

8. Anjuli Sastry and Karen Grigsby Bates. "When LA Erupted in Anger: A Look Back at the Rodney King Riots." *NPR: The Los Angeles Riots, 25 Years On*, 26 Apr. 2017, npr.org. Accessed 10 Jan. 2019.

9. Peter Feuerherd. "Why Didn't the Rodney King Video Lead to a Conviction?" *JSTOR Daily*, 28 Feb. 2018, daily.jstor.org. Accessed 10 Jan. 2019.

10. Jonathan Dienst et al. "Gunman Who Killed 2 NYPD Officers Wrote He Was 'Putting Wings on Pigs.'" *NBC 4 New York,* 20 Dec. 2014, nbcnewyork.com. Accessed 10 Jan. 2019.

11. "Justice Department Announces Findings of Two Civil Rights Investigations in Ferguson, Missouri." *Department of Justice Office of Public Affairs*, 4 Mar. 2015, justice.gov. Accessed 10 Jan. 2019.

12. Kate Wheeling. "How Many People Are Really Killed by Police in the United States?" *Pacific Standard*, 10 Oct. 2017, psmag.com. Accessed 10 Jan. 2019.

CHAPTER 7. LAW ENFORCEMENT AFTER 9/11

1. "FAQ about 9/11: What Happened on 9/11?" *9/11 Memorial & Museum*, n.d., 911memorial.org. Accessed 10 Jan. 2019.

2. "US Department of Homeland Security." USA.gov, n.d., usa.gov. Accessed 10 Jan. 2019.

3. "Police and Detectives: Work Environment." *Occupational Outlook Handbook, Bureau of Labor Statistics, US Department of Labor*, 13 Apr. 2018, bls.gov. Accessed 10 Jan. 2019.

4. "Injuries, Illness, Fatalities: Fact Sheet-Police Officers—August 2016." *Bureau of Labor Statistics, US Department of Labor*, 27 Apr. 2018, bls.gov. Accessed 10 Jan. 2019.

5. "2017 Law Enforcement Officers Killed & Assaulted: Officers Assaulted." *Federal Bureau of Investigation, Uniform Crime Reporting Program*. n.d., ucr.fbi.gov. Accessed 10 Jan. 2019.

6. Haley Hinkle and Rachel Levinson-Waldman. "The Abolish Ice Movement Explained." *Brennan Center for Justice*, 30 July 2018, brennancenter.org. Accessed 10 Jan. 2019.

7. Yarin Eski. *Policing, Port Security and Crime Control: An Ethnography of the Port Securityscape*. Routledge, 2016. 1. *Google Books*. Accessed 10 Jan. 2019.

CHAPTER 8. LAW ENFORCEMENT TODAY AND IN THE FUTURE

1. Barack Obama. "Remarks by the President at Memorial Service for Fallen Dallas Police Officers." *White House, President Barack Obama, Speeches and Remarks*, 12 July 2016, obamawhitehouse.archives.gov. Accessed 10 Jan. 2019.

2. "About NASRO." *National Association of School Resource Officers*, n.d., nasro.org. Accessed 10 Jan. 2019.

3. Brian A. Reaves. "Local Police Departments, 2013: Personnel, Policies, and Practices." *US Department of Justice, Office of Justice Programs, Bureau of Justice Statistics*, May 2015, bjs.gov. Accessed 10 Jan. 2019.

4. Jen Fifield. "Does Diversifying Police Forces Reduce Tensions?" *PEW*, 22 Aug. 2018, pewtrusts.org. Accessed 10 Jan. 2019.

5. "ShotSpotter Frequently Asked Questions." *ShotSpotter*, January 2018, shotspotter.com. Accessed 10 Jan. 2019.

6. "Frequently Asked Questions." *National Association of School Resource Officers*, n.d., nasro.org. Accessed 10 Jan. 2019.

7. Cindy Rodriguez. "New York's Kindest." *WNYC News*, 23 Dec. 2015, wnyc.org. Accessed 10 Jan. 2019.

8. Darren DaRonco and Carli Brosseau. "Many in Mental Crisis Call Tucson Police." *Arizona Daily Star*, 14 Apr. 2013, tucson.com. Accessed 10 Jan. 2019.

9. Booker Hodges. "2 Reasons Cops Should Not Respond to Non-Violent Mental Health Calls." *PoliceOne*, 22 Sept. 2017, policeone.com. Accessed 10 Jan. 2019.

10. R. L. Levenson Jr. et al. "The Badge of Life Psychological Survival for Police Officers Program." *International Journal of Emergency Mental Health*, vol. 2, issue 2, Spring 2010. *PubMed*, ncbi.nlm.nih.gov. Accessed 10 Jan. 2019.

11. Tessie Castillo. "What Is Law Enforcement Assisted Diversion (LEAD)?" *Huffington Post*, 26 May 2017, huffingtonpost.com. Accessed 10 Jan. 2019.

12. Hanna Kozlowska. "A Major Police Organization Has Issued a Formal Apology to Minorities for 'Historical Mistreatment.'" *Quartz*, 17 Oct. 2016, qz.com. Accessed 10 Jan. 2019.

INDEX

ABOUT THE AUTHORS

DUCHESS HARRIS, JD, PHD

Dr. Harris is a professor of American Studies at Macalester College and curator of the Duchess Harris Collection of ABDO books. She is also the coauthor of the titles in the collection, which features popular selections such as *Hidden Human Computers: The Black Women of NASA* and series including News Literacy and Being Female in America.

Before working with ABDO, Dr. Harris authored several other books on the topics of race, culture, and American history. She served as an associate editor for *Litigation News*, the American Bar Association Section of Litigation's quarterly flagship publication, and was the first editor in chief of *Law Raza*, an interactive online journal covering race and the law, published at William Mitchell College of Law. She has earned a PhD in American Studies from the University of Minnesota and a JD from William Mitchell College of Law.

REBECCA MORRIS

Rebecca Morris has a PhD in English from Texas A&M University. She is coeditor of *Representing Children in Chinese and U.S. Children's Literature* (Ashgate, 2014), a contributor to *Jacqueline Wilson* (ed. Lucy Pearson, Palgrave Macmillan New Casebooks, 2015), and the author of nonfiction books for students. Morris also writes literature guides for education websites.